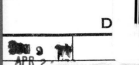

DIVIDED WE STAND

DIVIDED
WE STAND

*Reflections on the Crisis
at Cornell*

Edited by
Cushing Strout and David I. Grossvogel

Doubleday & Company, Inc., Garden City, New York, 1970

Library of Congress Catalog Card Number 79–116257
Copyright © 1970 by David I. Grossvogel and Cushing Strout
All Rights Reserved
Printed in the United States of America
First Edition

CONTENTS

EDITORS' NOTE

The problem that joins the writers in this volume is the fate of university life in a time of troubles. All historical writing is an effort to transcend history by an attempt to understand it, but so long as the historian himself is a committed participant in the process upon which he reflects, he is caught in the backwash of those events and marked by the shadows that those waves cast upon the present and future.[1] The history, the format, and the title of this book

[1] As this manuscript goes to the printer the madness continues. In the month following the tossing of a road flare, discovered unlit on the porch of the black girls' cooperative, a fire burned most of the Africana Center during the spring vacation of 1970, destroying private papers and a library of black studies. The administration and town authorities sponsored a voluntary restitution-fund. Members of the Black Liberation Front did $4,000 worth of damage to the new campus store. When the President learned that the Africana fire was officially attributed to arson, he replied to black demands for special safety and transportation measures, posted a reward, and sought federal investigatory help. Subsequently, members of the BLF did $30,000 worth of damage to windows, including those of the main library. The administration secured temporary restraining orders (vacated later) against black and white radical organizations and some individuals. Three white students were arrested in a brief small take-over of a nuclear lab. The library was again assaulted, this time by two Molotov cocktails that were put out. A guard said he saw two whites on the scene just after the throwing. There were repeated bomb-scare false alarms. A year after the events chronicled in this book, the faculty appears to be undivided in support of the President and the radicals have no mass base among the students.

document a festering sore: its original title, *Beyond Black and White,* and the hopes implicit in that title, were not to be realized. Some of our colleagues tried to persuade us not to "rock the boat" by writing about it; others, whose contributions we sought, objected to appearing in company with those whose position they opposed during the crisis. The price for the inclusion of the last article (an essential one) was the present two-part separation: even at the level of speculation we are sundered by the divisiveness of our times. The book was to have been *Beyond Black and White* not only because we do not think of the student revolution in Manichean terms, but also because we think that issues posed by the crisis at Cornell University transcend the racial politics of black and white.

With the exception of the preliminary piece by Professor Kahin, in whose words much of the passion and commitment of the Barton Hall days still endures, and which was included for that reason, our selection represents the reflective writing of people for whom campus events were a stimulus to later thought on the wider and deeper meaning of the issues. In most cases, the position of the writer during the events themselves adds a special interest to his observations. Professor Strout's essay presents a narrative of the crisis and its background in the context of the personal experience of a humanities professor actively involved in what was happening. It dramatizes the painful divisiveness that rends a campus when local issues become symbolic surrogates for political passions that profoundly disturb the larger society. The article by Professor Kenworthy discusses the political role and character of the vast majority of students brought together as a body under extraordinary circumstances during the crisis. From the perspective of a sympathetic observer and political participant, it analyzes the double role of the majority in both supporting and checking the pressures of the radical vanguard groups.

It is as a practicing psychiatrist and graduate student

in history that Dr. Feinstein evaluates his interviews of many actors in the April drama, investigating the emotional meaning of the breakdown of institutional authority. Within this microcosm, he traces the emergence of a "paranoid style" that other social scientists have noted in elements of our national politics. Finally, Professor Grossvogel analyzes in the utilitarianism of President Perkins' educational philosophy characteristics that have long left their impress on much of American higher education and notes how these humanitarian concerns coincide with the utilitarianism of the New Left that was directed against the ivory towers of traditional knowledge.

In Part II, Mr. Donald presents for the first time, from his position within the Black Liberation Front, a behind-the-scenes view of the black militants' tensions and tests that finally led to the seizure of a campus building whose occupation and surrender became front-page news throughout the country.

For the convenience of the reader we have prepared three chronologies. The first is a panoramic view of the spectrum of events over a three-year period. The second chronicles the details of the first major confrontation and the first issue of academic freedom raised by black protest at Cornell. The third focuses on the critical week of events stemming from the occupation by blacks of the student union building.

Any event in social history gives more prominence to some voices than to others. To some extent we have felt an obligation to redress that imbalance. We recognize that our book includes no administrative voice, though of course administrators have spoken in public about the crisis. The need for executive discretion, the pragmatic cast of Cornell administrators at the time, or the executive's concern for the corporate image in a public relations sense seemed to us good reasons for relying on faculty or student reflections for the kind of essay we wanted. Each of these writers has a point of view that is not typical of any campus orthodoxy or heresy, and in that marginality we hope there is insight.

The tactical question of whether or not the faculty should have voted as it did was widely debated on campus, particularly after the fact. Some still believe, in the language of a powerful presentation made at a meeting of the university faculty, that Cornell "can survive the expulsion or departure of no matter what numbers of students and the destruction of buildings far better than it can survive the death of principle." Others are convinced that a wobbly administration, armed students, inexperienced deputies, and the sentiments of several thousand students made it unwise to rely on an argument from principle divorced from the grim context of events. We do not think it is necessary to argue that there were decent and intelligent men who voted to nullify the judicial reprimands, refused to nullify them, or changed their minds from one meeting to the next. In any case we do not wish to center our attention on this issue, which has embittered too many collegial relations without doing much to illuminate the problems implicit in the crisis.

Our collection can serve one useful purpose if it breaks down the stereotypes of campus revolts. The "conservatives" see outside agitators or Communists, an "un-American" minority of anarchists or other bugaboos at the bottom of every upheaval. The "liberals" see rigid "uptight" bureaucrats frustrating ardent demands for the reform of archaic structures. White "radicals" see the "Establishment" as a mode of "political oppression" and black "radicals" see every problem in terms of the white's "innate" inability to understand the black. Each view basks in the glow of its own sense of virtue, relatively indifferent to the stubborn facts that do not fit into its framework. Each side tends to interpret campus events by analogy with the side it takes on questions of national politics, grotesquely inflating local and specific conflicts. The crisis at Cornell took place on a campus where the leading administrators prided themselves on being flexible, up to date, progressive. Yet it is also a campus where ROTC has stronger support in the faculty than it does among the students. Many of its students are from urban Eastern areas, but they are domiciled in a rural, upstate location. Its fourteen colleges include a Hotel School and a College of Agriculture as well as an Industrial and Labor Relations School and a College of Arts and Sciences. Some of them are state-supported, others are privately endowed. In 1969 Cornell's SDS chapter was the third largest in the country; there was still a fraternity system; and there were by then 250 black students on campus, most of them affiliated with the College of Arts and Sciences. This extraordinary mixture of elements at Cornell gives it a claim to a microcosmic significance. If any place could shatter the convenient stereotypes of campus revolution, surely Cornell would. To what extent it did, each reader will judge for himself.

Speaking for ourselves as editors, we know that the crises of the larger society are profoundly serious and we do not intend to minimize them by insisting, as we do, that the university has its own problems which cannot be dealt with as if they were only relevant aspects of larger issues. If this position, at this moment in our history, is already a partisan one, then we can only say: make the most of it. Our only criterion for inclusion was the capacity to write with acuity after fear and rancor had subsided, after sufficient time had passed to consider the problems of Cornell in a less parochial context.

C. S.

D. I. G.

CHRONOLOGIES

1. PANORAMIC CHRONOLOGY

1966: Black male cooperative house (Elmwood) established.
Inter-fraternity Judicial Board puts Phi Delta Theta on social probation for charging fee to some black students at dance.

Afro-American Society (AAS) votes to boycott "rushing."

1967: Black women's cooperative (WARI) established.

1968: March 19–April 4: Black students protest alleged "covert racism" of Professor Michael McPhelin, disrupt his class, and occupy office of chairman of department of economics. (For detailed chronology see following Close Up Chronology.)

April 5: Campus memorial services for Martin Luther King, Jr. Murder of King followed by several campus fires, including burning of the College chapel.

April 8: Special University Commission formed to investigate and "assess the respective responsibilities of all persons directly involved" in McPhelin affair.

April 22: Cornell Chapter of the Association of American University Professors complains to President that timing of formation of Special Commission and wording of its charge are contrary to established procedure giving professor right to judgment "by his peers and only by his peers."

April 26: Special Commission concludes that protest was "a serious interference with a professor's performance of his academic duties," that the freedom of chairman was restricted, and that handling of students' complaints was "far from satisfactory."

December 6–7: Forty black students proclaim themselves new Black Studies advisory committee and take possession of building, earlier scheduled for their use the next fall.

December 12: Several black students demonstrate with toy pistols and overturn vending machines.

December 13: Large group of black students conduct AAS demonstrations for autonomous degree-granting black college: sit in at President's office, run through clinic, dance on tables of student-union cafeteria, and remove large numbers of books from libraries' shelves to circulation desks.

1969: February 28: President Perkins is jerked from microphone by black student at conference on South Africa.

March 10: SDS breaks into Malott Hall to force end of recruiting for Chase Manhattan Bank.

March 12: University Faculty votes (306–229) to require appearance before Conduct Board of six black students involved in toy pistol incident or later taking of small items of furniture from a dormitory for AAS use. (No citations for the December 13 incidents.)

March 13: Over one hundred AAS members, not including six defendants, appear before Conduct Board and protest legitimacy of judicial system. Board drops its intended judgment of temporary suspension for students' non-appearance. Seeks advice of Faculty Committee on Student Affairs.

March 26: Faculty Committee on Student Affairs' response to AAS is published by campus newspaper in special supplement that supports Conduct Board's hearing of cases and requirement of defendants' appearance.

April 16: Faculty Committee on Student Affairs makes defendants' appearance before Conduct Board optional and instructs Board to act on pending cases.

April 18: Conduct Board issues reprimands to three black students and acquits two.

Series of false fire alarms.

Burning cross found on porch of black women's coop by Ithaca Police Detective.

April 19: Occupation of Willard Straight Hall. (For details see following Close Up Chronology.)

April 21: President's emergency proclamation.

President's Convocation speech at Barton Hall.

University Faculty at Bailey Hall votes (726–281) for President's seven points.

April 22: All-night mass meeting of students in Barton Hall.

April 23: University Faculty nullifies reprimands and votes for restructuring proposal.

President joins mass meeting at Barton Hall.

Chairman of department of government submits resignation in protest against "changed context."

April 24: Professor of government resigns in protest against loss of academic freedom.

Professor of history resigns from chairmanship of department.

About twenty professors of history and government say they will cease normal teaching activity until all firearms removed from campus.

April 25: Teach-in on academic freedom at Barton Hall.

April 27: Forty-one professors warn of dangers to academic freedom and standards.

May 1: SDS paints cannon in Barton Hall.
Trustees announce guidelines and support President.
Ten SDS demonstrators to be booked for trespass.

May 2: University Faculty votes for Constituent Assembly and for committee to delineate functions and duties of Faculty.

May 14: City Court charges eighteen black students with trespass.

May 31: President instructs Trustees to search for successor.
First meeting of Constituent Assembly.

June 2: Black professor of economics resigns, charging Cornell with academic favoritism to black students.
Black honors graduate of Central Michigan University and Ph.D. candidate at Northwestern University accepts directorship of Center for Afro-American Studies, funded and approved by Trustees on April 12.

2. CHRONOLOGY OF EVENTS RELATED TO ECONOMICS 103, SPRING SEMESTER, 1968*

This was the setting for the events of March 19–April 4.

The following chronology is based solely upon testimony heard by the Special Commission, and is not intended to be complete, nor precise in all details. In particular, all statements concerning particular individuals are based upon uncontradicted testimony, but the Commission has not made any additional investigation of validity or accuracy.

January 30:

> Opening Lecture: discussion of nature of Economics characterized as originating in Western thought. "Economic development" described as essentially a product of Western civilization. Two black students note negative reactions, feeling lecture is "racist" in tone.

February–
March 14:

> Other lectures, from time to time, during several weeks touched on cultural differences, differences in climate, resources, and characteristic values and behavior-patterns. Several references to differences between temperate and tropical cultures apparently exacerbated the feeling of some black students.

*From the Report of the Special Commission on the McPhelin incident, April 26, 1968.

March 14:
(Thursday)

Certain black students react strongly against references to urban poor people in lecture in Economics 103 in connection with description of conditions accompanying poverty.

March 19:
(Tuesday)

In lecture on poverty, Professor McPhelin refers to social conditions in slums, including a passing characterization of children's games as "sick and perverse." Later, when a question from one of the black students (Mr. Marshall John Garner), challenging the relevance of a comparison of educational levels over time, is reiterated, the question is ignored. At the end of the lecture Professor McPhelin asks Mr. Garner to come to the desk, and then apologizes for ignoring the student's question. When Mr. Garner insists that a private apology is not adequate, Professor McPhelin promises to apologize to the entire class at the next meeting on March 21 (Thursday).

March 20:
(Wednesday)

Thereafter Messrs. Garner, Rone and Cooper decide to take a complaint to the Vice President for Student Affairs. Mr. Barlow is not in his office and the students are referred by a secretary to the Associate Dean Stanley Levy in the Office of the Dean of Students, to whom the students tell their grievance. Mr. Levy refers them to Dean Brown of the College of Arts and Sciences. Mr. Levy does not talk directly to Brown, but has his secretary try to arrange the appointment with Dean Brown's secretary. Mr. Levy did not communicate with either Professor McPhelin or Chairman Davis, judging the matter one for academic channels only.

March 20:
(Continued)

When Dean Brown is told simply that some students want to discuss Economics 103, he asks his secretary to arrange an appointment for them to see Chairman Davis at 11:00 a.m. However, it is not possible to reach the students to tell them to go directly to the Department of Economics.

When three students appear at Dean Brown's door, he decides to talk with them. The students state their complaints and demand that the professor be dismissed, that he make a public apology, and that a black economist be brought in to give "the other side." Dean Brown seeks to advise them concerning procedural due process as regards a professor; he also has his secretary reconfirm their appointment with Professor Davis, and tells the students that he sees no problem regarding the outside speaker, although this is a decision to be made by the Department of Economics.

The three students attempt to have an immediate meeting with Chairman Davis. Apparently there was a misunderstanding as to definiteness of the appointment supposedly arranged through Dean Brown's secretary. Professor Davis is in an examination which is continuing longer than expected, and his secretary makes a tentative appointment for the students to see him at 1:30 p.m. on March 21.

March 20:
(Wednesday
evening)

Professor Davis, by an appointment fixed five weeks earlier, has dinner with Professor McPhelin, and tells the latter of his forthcoming appointment with the students. Professor McPhelin tells Mr. Davis that the problem may have derived from his remarks in the "poverty lecture," that he had cut off Garner's question about the relevance of longitudinal statistics on education, that he had apologized after class and would apologize at the next meeting of the whole class (meeting 10:10 a.m. on March 21).

March 21:
(Thursday)

Professor McPhelin makes apology to class for ignoring student's question on March 19.

March 21:
(Thursday)

Professor Davis expects black students at 1:30 p.m., according to note on his calendar, but no one appears, or calls to explain absence. He assumes that classroom apology has been made and accepted and that nothing more will be heard of the matter.

March 22–
April 1:

Spring Recess, and resumption of instruction. No further developments known to faculty or administration.

April 1:
(Monday)

Appointment made for meeting on following day between Professor Davis and four students from Economics 103.

April 2:
(Tuesday)

Meeting of Messrs. Bertram Cooper, Marshall John Garner, Robert Rone and one other student with Professor Davis. Students present oral complaint. There is an exchange of views. Professor Davis finally replies that "nothing will be done." Students abruptly terminate conversation and depart.

April 3:
(Wednesday
evening)

Meeting of students of the Afro-American Society.
Messrs. Garner, Cooper, and Rone are present, as is
Assistant Dean of Students Gloria I. Joseph, for some
portion of the meeting. Among other items considered,
the grievances of the three students are reviewed. There
is no record of what additional information, if any, was
made available at this time to the students concerning
University procedures for complaints of this nature.

April 4:
(Thursday)

At the beginning of class in Economics 103, the complainants appear with their statement and ask Professor
McPhelin to allow them to read it to the entire class.
Professor McPhelin asks to read it privately first, and
is told that instead he may read a copy while the
students' spokesman simultaneously reads it to the class.
Professor McPhelin refuses, declaring that he "runs the
show." The spokesman insists upon reading the statement to the class, and does so. Disorder follows, and the
professor dismisses the class.

Apparently the three complainants then went to Willard
Straight Hall, from whence within several minutes they
returned along with some fifty to sixty others—mostly
black students but including some whites. The entire
group moved in a body to the offices of the Department
of Economics.

At approximately 10:30–10:40 a.m., a large number
of students enter the two main offices of the Department
of Economics, posting a notice on the outer door that
the office is temporarily closed. Three secretaries and
Professor Davis are within the offices. One of the black
students hands Professor Davis a statement of the com-

plaint and states that the offices are closed and the
students would remain until Professor Davis agrees to
arrange a meeting with someone who could act upon
their demands. (For some time—fifteen to twenty minutes—the situation appeared to Professor Davis to be
chaotic, with much noise and simultaneous talking.)
Telephones are used by students, without permission, to
make calls to the New York *Times* and elsewhere.
Office secretaries are not allowed to answer incoming
calls. One secretary—needing medicine from her purse
in a desk drawer, is at first denied access by one student;
another student intervenes and the secretary is allowed
to obtain the medicine.

After an interval, the secretaries leave the offices.

Professor Davis declines invitations to call University
officers in Day Hall, until he has full use of his office.
A lengthy impasse follows.

Some students leave to obtain food and drinks. Attempts
by plainclothes members of the Safety Section to prevent
their re-entrance are followed by violence. After this
altercation, no further attempts are made to regain official
control by Safety Section personnel.

At some time after noon, Dean Miller of the University
Faculty talks by telephone with Professor Davis, and is
told that a discussion would not be useful at that point.
At another time, Mr. Lowell George, Supervisor of the
Safety Section, signals Professor Davis through a window,
asking if he wishes forcible measures taken to release
him; Professor Davis demurs. (The latter testified that
"my estimate was that this would lead to violence.") At
several subsequent times Mr. George repeats the offer.
Professor Davis makes no attempt to leave the office; he
testifies that in his judgment such an attempt would
not have been successful. As time passes, Professor
Davis feels that the atmosphere is improving. At a point
later in the afternoon one of the participants chooses to

leave to see the Provost. Professor Davis is allowed to
go to another part of the building accompanied by three
members of the group. After he leaves the office, Provost
Corson and other University personnel enter.

Informal negotiations follow, in which it apparently
is agreed that an outside speaker with a different view
would be brought to Cornell at Department expense, but
with no assurance that the speaker would address
Professor McPhelin's class during a class hour. The
agreement apparently permits the speaker to be "of the
Society's choosing." Also agreed upon is a meeting to
be held with Dean Brown, who is then out of town, on
the following Monday, April 8.

April 6:
(Saturday)

Meeting of Dean Brown and Professors McPhelin and
Davis. Reference is made to the repeated interchanges
during the semester with Mr. Garner; no decisions for
further action are recorded as having been made by the
three participants.

April 6–8:

Various meetings of University officers, faculty, students;
decision to form Special Commission.

April 8:
(Monday)

Organization of the Commission.

April 9:
(Tuesday)

All University classes suspended. Economics 103 lecture not held.

April 11:
(Thursday)

Professor McPhelin resumes lecturing in Economics 103.
He omits the topic originally scheduled for April 4 and

hence carried over to April 11. That topic was, racial aspects of poverty, which had appeared in his original course outline. He omitted it because he "was advised to stay off it."

April 10–17:

Hearings of the Commission.

April 18–25:

Drafting of report of the Commission.

April 26:

Submission of final report of the Commission.

3. A CHRONOLOGICAL REPORT: FRIDAY MORNING, APRIL 18, THROUGH WEDNESDAY AFTERNOON, APRIL 23, 1969*

More than four months after the events of December 12, the Conduct Board finally handed down reprimands to three of the black students and acquitted two. The sixth student cited had withdrawn from the University. These decisions were reached and announced at 2:00 A.M. on Friday, April 18.

The next significant event occurred shortly thereafter at Wari House, 208 Dearborn Place, a cooperative for sophomores, juniors, and senior women whose admissions to Cornell have been sponsored by COSEP (Committee on Special Educational Projects). Eleven coeds resided there. Miss Charisse Cannady, a senior and head resident there, was awakened by a brick thrown at a window in her bedroom on the ground floor of the frame house. She quickly went to the window and saw a burning cross on the front porch steps. At 2:53 A.M. she pulled the fire alarm in the building. After seeing that all the girls were aroused and safe, she gathered them in the kitchen and, being well aware of the racial overtones of this burning cross, had the girls lie on the floor.

Police from three sources were promptly at the scene: City of Ithaca, Cornell Division of Safety and Security, and Cayuga Heights. A city detective who was patrolling nearby reached the scene almost immediately, found the cross burning on the steps, and removed it to the front yard. He and a Cornell

* From the trustees' report on *Campus Unrest at Cornell*, September 5, 1969.

campus patrolman smothered the fire. The police action took only about four minutes from the time Miss Cannady turned in the alarm at 2:53 A.M. Beginning at 2:57 A.M. there were three fire alarms set off within a two-minute period from three of the women's large dormitories—Donlon, Dickson, and Risley Halls.

The Ithaca and campus police were ordered to report immediately to these dormitories, which housed many coeds. The burning cross had been quickly extinguished. The Cayuga Heights patrolman did not go to these other alarms since the dormitories are all located within the City of Ithaca. He returned to his regular patrol route and continued to check 208 Dearborn Place periodically.

All three of these alarms were false; they were among eleven such false alarms set off in University buildings between 1:43 and 5:08 A.M. Officials have no knowledge of who set off any of these false alarms or of the purpose behind this irresponsible action.

According to Safety Division records, at 3:20 A.M., less than a half hour after the cross-burning was first discovered, a campus patrolman returned to 208 Dearborn Place and remained there until 3:40 A.M. when he was relieved by another campus patrolman who policed the premises until later in the morning.

At 3:30 A.M. Mrs. Ruth Darling, associate dean of students, telephoned the Safety Division because Miss Cannady had called her requesting protection for Wari House. The campus patrolman on duty apparently had not made known his presence to the residents. He was instructed to do so and did immediately, before being relieved at 3:40 A.M.

At approximately 5:30 A.M., with the first light of day, two men from the Safety Division went to 208 Dearborn Place and took pictures of the window which had been broken, of the steps where the cross had been burning, and of some footprints which were found outside. The cross itself was about six feet long and three feet wide and had been wrapped in white cloth, which had not been completely burned. It was later determined that the wood came from the Campus Store, being sold there frequently for use in art courses. There is no official knowledge of who may have been responsible for the cross-burning.

The long-standing resentment over the slow progress of the black studies program, plus the recent decisions against the blacks by a judicial system whose validity they did not recognize, followed closely by the cross-burning at Wari House—these were the apparent irritants which led to the take-over of Willard Straight Hall. The blacks, numbering between fifty and one hundred (the estimates vary widely), entered Willard Straight Hall at approximately 5:30 A.M. Saturday, April 19. This was Parents Weekend at Cornell and the blacks indicated that they planned the building take-over for that weekend to make their plight known to the parents. They chose Willard Straight Hall because, particularly on a weekend such as this, there is a high level of activity in the building, involving many students. The take-over of the building would interfere with the lives of many, thus publicizing their cause to a very great extent.

From the black students themselves, it was learned that there were more women than men in the group taking over the building. There were also about ten non-students from downtown Ithaca, believed to have been of high school age, in Willard Straight at least part of the time during its occupation.

The blacks immediately began their take-over by securing the building, removing the employees from the building, and then the overnight guests. There were three groups of blacks who had been assigned to clear the building of its occupants: one group to handle the house department employees, another the dining employees, and the third the guests.

The Safety Division received the first word from the employees at 5:38 A.M., notifying them that the building was

being seized by some blacks. The first calls to the Safety
Division from guests came at 5:48 A.M. The Safety Division
told people to lock their doors but later indicated to the
guests that they should not resist and should follow the
directions of the blacks. There were about thirty guests occupying the bedrooms of Willard Straight Hall that night,
mostly parents who were there for Parents Weekend.

These guests were awakened, given ten minutes to dress,
pack up, and leave. They were dealt with firmly, reasonably
politely, and courteously, although there were reports by
guests of several unpleasant experiences, none physical. The
guests were led down the main stairway through the Memorial
Room, down the back service stairway to the basement, and
out of the building from a loading dock on the west side of
the building.

The guests were asked to pack their bags, but in the confusion some left without packing all of their belongings. Later
that day arrangements were made so that the guests received
their property, with apparently no significant losses reported.

Although one or two of those ejected said that they saw
several guns and at least one white girl, most guests and employees reported seeing no such weapons and no whites. It is
felt by the Committee that the take-over was led by members of the Afro-American Society, who entered the building without guns, and no whites were among them.

Among those originally entering the building, a group
carried a large supply of wire, chains, and rope with which
to secure the entrances to the building. This work was quickly
completed and by shortly before 6:15 A.M. all persons except the blacks were out of the building, and it was secured.

The campus patrol arrived before 6:00 A.M. and verified
that the east and west doors were secured from within the
building. They assisted the guests and employees who had
been evicted, taking or guiding them to Sage Graduate
Center. The campus police on duty in front and in back
were instructed to inform persons approaching Willard Straight

of the take-over and not to allow anyone to attempt to enter the building. At about 6:30 A.M. a black couple came up the hill, verified that the building was taken over, and asked to go in and join the occupants. Eugene Dymek, director of the Safety Division, ordered his men to permit blacks to enter the building. The policy of the Safety Division was thus established. The building was not to be closed off, nor isolated. Whites were not to enter, but to be steered away. Blacks, however, might come and go at will.

At 7:05 A.M. a group of about fifty SDS members arrived from Anabel Taylor Hall and began picketing in front of the building in support of the blacks' action. At the request of the police, they stayed off the main sidewalk on Central Avenue. About one hour later they were carrying signs. Later in the day the SDS group had grown to around 150. They indicated that they would protect the blacks in Willard Straight from any attacks by white student groups.

Between 7:30 and 8:00 A.M. Vice Provost Keith Kennedy tried unsuccessfully to talk on the telephone with Edward Whitfield, president of the Afro-American Society. At approximately 9:15 A.M. University Counsel Neal Stamp, Safety Division Director Dymek, and Kennedy appeared in front of the building, asking to speak with Whitfield. When Whitfield appeared at the window, Kennedy asked to talk with him in person. Whitfield said that he would discuss the request with his colleagues. When he failed to appear, Dymek, on Stamp's instructions, took a bullhorn, identified himself, and demanded the evacuation of the building. This order was repeated several times as Dymek walked around the building.

At about 9:35 A.M. about twenty-five white students, mostly, if not all, from the DU fraternity (Delta Upsilon), tried to gain admission to the Straight through a window with a broken pane on the south side ground level of the building. This window leads into the studio of WVBR, a student-operated radio station. Of this group approximately a dozen entered the building, and some of them got as far as the bottom of the steps leading to the Ivy Room. Here they were met and turned back by the black men and forced to leave by the same window they entered. Three whites and one black were injured in the melee; all were treated at the Gannett Clinic next door. None of the injuries were regarded as particularly serious. Harsh words and threats were exchanged inside and outside while the whites were retreating.

The DU's were able to gain access to the building despite the policy set up by the campus patrol that whites should stay away because all seven campus police on duty at the Straight at this time were guarding the front and rear doors. There was none stationed on either the north or south sides of the building.

Whatever the motives were that brought on this action by the DU students, the abortive attempt to gain entrance was ill-conceived and irresponsible in the minds of this Committee. Certainly, this act was an important contributing factor to the blacks' growing fear of reprisal by the whites for the building take-over. This fear apparently was a major cause of the later introduction of arms.

At 8:00 A.M. that Saturday, the members of the University administration who were in Ithaca began their deliberations. Stamp first met with President Perkins in his office in Day Hall. Because of rumors of a possible take-over of Day Hall by SDS to show sympathy for the blacks, this meeting was moved before 8:30 A.M. to the White Art Museum where these men were joined by Kennedy, Controller Arthur H. Peterson, Vice Presidents Mark Barlow and Steven Muller, and by Dymek and Lowell T. George of the Safety Division. Faculty Trustees W. David Curtiss and Royse P. Murphy were present by invitation. Dale R. Corson, then University provost, and Robert Miller, dean of the Faculty, were in New York City and returned to Ithaca early Saturday evening. Stuart Brown, vice president for academic affairs, remained in Day Hall.

The discussion at the meeting in the Andrew Dickson

White Study turned to the use of the court injunction. Stamp emphasized that the blacks occupying Willard Straight would have to be ordered to leave before an injunction could be used. It was at this time that it was decided that Stamp, Kennedy and Dymek should go to the Straight and make their demands that the blacks leave as stated above.

President Perkins had indicated that without discussion with representative groups of faculty and students, he did not want to recommend police force, such as could result from an injunction. In this manner, should police action be necessary, he hoped to avoid the bitterness generated by the administration at Harvard, which reportedly decided on the forceful eviction of the radical students from University Hall without either consultation or notice to its faculty or students.

Because there has been no student government at Cornell since the student body voted to abolish it in 1968, the task of consulting with a representative student group was made most difficult, if not really impossible. Therefore, it was decided by the administration that the Faculty Council should meet, and Acting Dean of the Faculty Ernest F. Roberts, Jr., convened this meeting at 11:00 A.M. in Myron Taylor Hall. Many members of the Faculty Council were away that weekend. By prearrangement six additional faculty members were invited to attend, as well as eight students chosen from a list of volunteers submitted by Vice President for Student Affairs Barlow. Members of the administration sat in on this meeting. This group expressed a strong sentiment for the settlement of this take-over without the use of violence. They awaited the demands from the AAS which Whitfield had promised Kennedy at 11:30 A.M. These were finally delivered to Kennedy at 12:30 P.M., just after the Faculty Council had adjourned for lunch.

Earlier that morning, at 9:00 A.M., President Perkins was scheduled to talk to the Parents Weekend group in Alice Statler Auditorium. There were rumors that the SDS might try to take over that building or have an unpleasant confrontation with the President. It was decided that Barlow should represent the President on that occasion.

After the DU incident, retaliatory feeling among the white students was running high. Vice President Muller went on the air over station WVBR asking students to remain calm —to cool it! Elmer Meyer, Jr., dean of students and assistant vice president for student affairs, and his assistant, Albert Miles, went to Noyes Student Center to talk reason with a group of students, mostly fraternity men who had gathered there after the DU's had been ejected from the Straight. This meeting turned into an IFC (Interfraternity Council) meeting. They elected a representative to the meeting of the Faculty Council and agreed to have him request of that group an injunction against the black students occupying Willard Straight Hall.

The demands of the AAS were three in number: 1) that the judicial action against the five black students be nullified; 2) that the University reopen housing negotiations; and 3) that a full investigation of the cross-burning at Wari House be undertaken. Later that afternoon the demand regarding housing was dropped, but the third was amended to include an investigation of the attack by the DU group.

At 1:00 P.M. a meeting of the IFC Steering Committee was held. A statement drawn up by this group was ratified by the full IFC, 43 to 2, at 2:00 P.M. The statement opposed the use of the injunction or the intervention of civil authorities because they felt it would lead to further violence.

At 3:30 P.M. the augmented Faculty Council reconvened in Myron Taylor Hall, together with some members of the administration. They deliberated over the demands made by the blacks, control of fraternity groups, the DU incident, and ways of dislodging the students. It was agreed that for the time being there would be no injunction and police would not be summoned. It was decided that Acting Dean Roberts and Kennedy should talk with Whitfield, the AAS president.

They went to the Straight and discussed with Whitfield various options, such as appealing the cases against the blacks to the Student Faculty Appellate Board. This he rejected as implying recognition of the validity of that judicial system. This talk led to no agreement or progress toward one.

A large part of Saturday, Stamp had been working on the papers to request a court injunction, and he had been in contact with police and court officials.

Saturday afternoon at one o'clock the SDS held a meeting at Anabel Taylor Hall where they discussed plans for the seizure of Day Hall. That evening at eight-thirty the IFC and SDS sponsored a teach-in in Bailey Hall. There was strong sentiment for the blacks among these students, the feeling being that the judicial system had broken down in the handling of their case. IFC representatives made a strong pro-black statement which was received with cheers.

There was much informal action by small groups all day long and rumors were steadily growing in number. There had been a strong feeling of resentment between many blacks and whites prior to the cross-burning. There was resentment by many in the campus community over lack of discipline applied to violations of the conduct code by black militants and other activists. The unsolved muggings by blacks (not known whether students or non-students) and the rumored purchase of guns and ammunition by both blacks and whites all contributed to tense racial feeling on the campus before the take-over of the building. The seizure and the incident of the DU students obviously made the campus even more tense. And so the rumors had an atmosphere of distrust and fear in which to grow and spread. The Dean of Students' office set up a rumor clinic to which anyone might call to check the veracity of a story or rumor as he heard it. This office, with three phones, was used constantly and, without doubt, had a calming effect.

The planning by the blacks included a communication

system after they had taken over the building. They had the use of telephones. They also had brought along intercom equipment and could talk with observers outside whom they had placed in strategic locations on the campus. The result was that the blacks heard these rumors and such threats as: 1) a bomb was to go off in Willard Straight Hall; 2) the Wari House was to be burned; 3) a group of fraternity men were gathering at Noyes Lodge, drinking, and were organizing to attack the Straight. From time to time reports came in that other groups were collecting with arms to drive up to the Straight and "get back their building." The blacks had made a bold move in taking over the building. They had had time to think about it, and they knew that there was strong feeling on the campus. Witnesses agreed that they became truly frightened.

At eight that night President Perkins met at his home with members of his staff. Roberts, Barlow and Kennedy were present and shortly were joined by Dean of the Faculty Miller and Provost Corson, who had just returned from New York City. At about 9:00 P.M. they received a call from Whitfield inquiring about a rumor that eight carloads of students with guns were coming toward Willard Straight. Whitfield wanted to know what the University was going to do about it. Roberts checked with the Safety Division which confirmed that there was such a rumor, but stated that they could find no substance behind it. The administration tried to reach Whitfield to pass on this information, but the lines were tied up and they were unable to get through to him.

This meeting at the President's house was just breaking up at about 10:15 P.M. when word was received that between 9:45 and 10:00 P.M. the campus patrolmen on duty behind Willard Straight had observed blacks taking guns into Willard Straight Hall.

At 10:30 P.M. Kennedy went to the Safety Division and telephoned Whitfield. Whitfield admitted the presence of arms in the Straight. He said they were only for protection; the blacks had no confidence that the campus patrol would protect them from the threatened attacks by the whites. Kennedy tried to persuade him to have the blacks leave the building, and he offered to bring buses around to take them home. The answer was negative. He then requested Whitfield to bring the guns out and put them in the trunk of Kennedy's car. Whitfield hesitated quite a while and finally turned down this request.

As he left Perkins's home, Provost Corson commented, "It's a new ballgame." He also went to the Safety Division headquarters, where he stayed until a bomb threat to Barton Hall forced him to leave. While the rumor about the bomb was coming in, there were false alarms, a bad fire at the Chi Psi Fraternity house (actually two separate fires of suspicious origin, although the Ithaca Fire Department has decided that arson was not involved); and a rumored sniper in the Library Tower who turned out to be a night watchman replacing a light bulb in the tower. There were rumors of carloads of white students roaming the campus with guns. These were never confirmed. Corson later reported to the Board of Trustees at their special May 1 meeting that he was most concerned about the possibilities of getting through that night without serious trouble.

At 7:30 A.M. Sunday the SDS held a meeting in Anabel Taylor to plan a rally later that morning. They resumed their picketing of Willard Straight Hall.

At 9:00 A.M. President Perkins and some members of his executive staff met in Myron Taylor Hall. There followed sharp discussion of the alternatives for action. There was a sense of the necessity to remove the blacks that day, as they feared for the ability of the campus to remain peaceful another night. Finally Dean Miller offered the suggestion that he call a meeting of the University faculty on Monday and recommend nullification of the decisions against the blacks, provided the blacks leave the Straight immediately.

The news of the guns was out. It was heard over the air early that morning. The press kept asking Director of Public Information Thomas L. Tobin, "What are you going to do about the guns?"

The expanded Faculty Council, now grown to twenty-five, met at 11:00 A.M. in Myron Taylor. Corson, Roberts, Perkins and Miller attended this meeting, or portions of it.

At the staff meeting it was decided that Kennedy should call Whitfield. The latter thought it might be useful to talk. It was finally decided by the group that Muller accompany Kennedy. There was considerable discussion as to the advisability of Miller's proposal. Some felt that the faculty would not rescind the decisions, and the reaction of the blacks to this further rejection would be serious. The President returned from the Faculty Council meeting and held phone calls with Trustees Robert W. Purcell and Jansen Noyes, Jr. Later he insisted that there must be quid pro quo agreement by which the blacks would agree to help in deciding on a new judicial system and would abide by it when adopted.

At twelve noon Muller and Kennedy left for Willard Straight. It had been agreed that they would talk with the blacks and that the points of discussion would be:

1. The University would investigate the cross-burning and the DU incidents
2. Miller would call a faculty meeting and recommend nullification
3. The blacks must leave the building right away
4. The blacks must help in building a viable and acceptable judicial system

A black law student, Barry Loncke, who had been talking with Whitfield earlier, warning the blacks of the legal problems they had created for themselves, was in the conference along with Whitfield and another black, Bob Jackson, plus Kennedy and Muller. Muller stated that their goal was to get the blacks to leave the building as quickly as possible.

Whitfield asked that the faculty meeting be held right away while they still occupied the building, rather than on Monday. This was rejected. The blacks must leave the building first. He raised the question of refusal by the faculty to nullify and was told that all that Miller could do was recommend the nullification. The vote was up to the faculty.

After thirty to forty minutes of discussion, Kennedy and Muller left, returning to Myron Taylor Hall. There the President, with members of his executive staff, continued the discussions. They agreed that the University not provide legal services to the black students. Stamp left before 1:00 P.M. to go downtown to arrange for, and be prepared to use, a court injunction if, later, that was decided on. He arranged a meeting with a number of city officials, as well as state police, for 2:00 P.M. in the office of Mayor Jack K. Kiely. He kept in touch by telephone with Corson at the Law School.

During this period Kennedy talked to Whitfield by phone. Whitefield also talked with Miller and asked if he was prepared to call the faculty meeting and recommend nullification. Miller replied that he was prepared to do so if they got out of the building right away. Miller stated to Whitfield that if the faculty refused to nullify the penalties he would resign as dean of the faculty. On his later return to the meeting of the expanded Faculty Council, Miller repeated this promise made to Whitfield.

Muller had the main points of agreement typed up. He and Kennedy returned to Willard Straight shortly after 3:00 P.M. They met with Whitfield, Jackson, Zachary Carter (vice chairman of AAS) and a few others. In addition to a discussion of the points to be covered in the agreement, the question of the role of the SDS in their leaving the building came up. It was decided that the group of 150 SDS who were picketing outside should be asked to leave, and the blacks arranged this. Finally, the subject of the guns came up. Muller and Kennedy asked that they be left behind, but

Whitfield insisted that they were needed for protection. After considerable discussion, because they wanted to get the students out as quickly as possible, it was determined that the blacks were to leave with their guns, unloaded, and with breeches open. At no time during the negotiations did the blacks threaten these men with their weapons. In fact, the blacks, according to Muller and Kennedy, were at all times respectful, though grim and determined.

Muller had talked with Corson and reported that the blacks were insisting that they leave with their guns. Stamp, still at the mayor's office, learned of this and he reported that the officials downtown, city and state police, were very upset about this situation.

The entire group in the Straight was delayed while the blacks cleaned up the building. It had been agreed that the blacks, with Kennedy and Muller, would walk over to 320 Wait Avenue, headquarters for the AAS, and that the pact would be signed there.

At 4:10 P.M. the front doors of Willard Straight opened and out came 120 black students, many of them brandishing guns, with Muller and Kennedy. A large group, estimated at two thousand, had gathered as word spread of the pending evacuation of the building. As the blacks emerged, a loud cheer went up, but they themselves remained silent as they marched across the campus to their headquarters at 320 Wait Avenue.

It was during this exit and march that the press and television representatives took the pictures which were seen around the world and gave such an ugly impression of the event.

At 320 Wait Avenue, shortly before 5:00 P.M., after the agreement had been put in its final form, it was signed by Kennedy, Muller, Whitfield, and Zachary Carter. Whitfield read and signed it outside before a large gathering of onlookers and the press.

The pact read as follows:

AGREEMENT BETWEEN THE AAS AND CORNELL
RELATING TO BLACK STUDENT DEPARTURE
FROM WILLARD STRAIGHT HALL

PART I

In a meeting to be held 21 April 1969 the Dean of the Cornell Faculty, Robert D. Miller, will recommend to the full faculty that the judicial procedures taken against the five students as a result of incidents last December and January be nullified by action of the full faculty.

PART II

The University promises best efforts to secure legal assistance to defend against any civil actions arising out of the occupation of Willard Straight by the AAS. Such efforts will be made on behalf of individuals or the group.

PART III

The University will press no civil or criminal charges, or take any measures to punish by means of expulsion or otherwise, activities of the AAS involved in occupation of WSH. The University will assume all responsibility for damages to WSH.

PART IV

The University will provide 24-hour protection for 208 Dearborn Place (Women's Co-op) and 320 Wait, with men assigned this task at all times.

PART V

The University undertakes to investigate thoroughly police activities related to both the burning of the cross incident and the attack on Willard Straight Hall by unknown individuals. A detailed report will be issued to the AAS and made public including identities of those involved.

PART VI

The AAS has discontinued the occupation of Willard
Straight Hall.

PART VII

The AAS undertakes to cooperate in devising a new judiciary system to promote justice on Cornell's campus for
all members of the student body.

Signed on 20 April 1969

FOR THE UNIVERSITY	FOR THE AAS
Steven Muller	Ed Whitfield
VICE PRESIDENT	CHAIRMAN
W. K. Kennedy	Zachary W. Carter
VICE PROVOST	VICE CHAIRMAN

Damage done by the blacks during the take-over of Willard Straight at first was believed to have been minimal.
Unfortunately, a thorough survey estimated the total costs to
be approximately $10,800. This included food used or spoiled,
property damages, and labor to restore the building to full
use. Included in this was the cost of $2,000 for replacing
all locks and keys in the building, as the blacks had taken
the master keys from employees. They also broke off a
number of billiard cues to use the butts as clubs to defend
themselves. The total cost of this item was $1,780. In addition
to this expense of $10,800, it was estimated that there was
loss of business of $15,000 over the three-day period as
Willard Straight had to remain closed until Tuesday morning.
What the profit loss from this amount of business would have
been was not in this estimate, but obviously it would have
been relatively high since the overhead items, including labor,
had to be paid regardless of the occupation of the building.
It would be almost impossible to chronicle with accuracy
the numerous events that transpired on the three succeeding

days through Wednesday. This report will cover only the highlights in the order of their occurrence.

On Monday morning at nine-fifteen President Perkins issued his first statement since the building occupation. He announced that firearms were banned from the campus, with violators facing automatic suspension. Anyone involved in a building occupation would experience the same penalty.

At 12:15 P.M., in a further statement, he declared a state of emergency on the campus, and established an advisory board, with himself as chairman. He also assumed full authority and responsibility for the maintenance of safety and security. In so doing he acted on the authority vested in the President, and with the full agreement of the Board of Trustees chairman. He announced that the regulations covering the prohibition of firearms and building occupancies were being drafted. He also called a convocation for Barton Hall for 3:00 P.M. before the University Faculty meeting at 4:30 P.M., and he invited all members of the campus community to attend.

The convocation brought together in Barton Hall at 3:00 P.M. a crowd estimated at twelve thousand students, faculty, University employees, and interested Ithacans. The President in his talk, which lasted about twenty minutes, made no reference to the events on campus of the previous two-and-a-half days, asking all to approach the days ahead as humane men.

The University Faculty meeting was called to order at 4:40 P.M. in Bailey Hall, with 1,100 faculty members in attendance. After a statement by President Perkins, Dean Miller moved for the nullification of the judicial procedures taken against the blacks. After a long discussion, a seven-point motion introduced by President Perkins was substituted, which refused to agree at that time to dismiss the penalties but directed the AAS representatives to meet with the Faculty Council the next day and report at a faculty meeting on Friday. This substitute motion was passed. As a result of this failure of the faculty to vote on the dean of the faculty's motion for dismissal of the penalties, Miller, as he had promised the blacks on Sunday, announced his resignation as dean.

The news of the faculty decision spread fast. As the faculty was leaving Bailey, the SDS moved into the hall, along with two thousand students. This group voted to remain active until the demands of AAS were met.

Tuesday was a day of frenzied activity on the campus. The threats and rumors had started up again Monday night. The action by the faculty on Monday afternoon was interpreted by the students as rejection of nullification, whereas it was meant as a postponement of any decision, as the faculty did not want to decide under coercion. Postponement meant delay and to the students delay was unacceptable. Many groups met. The faculties of several colleges voted to approve nullification. Finally, the Faculty Council on Tuesday evening at 7:25 voted to recommend nullifying the penalties and called another faculty meeting for Wednesday at 12:15 P.M. in Bailey Hall.

At 6:00 P.M. Tom Jones (a member of the Afro-American Society) gave a lengthy talk over the local radio station, ending up threatening Perkins, four top administrators, and three professors, and "giving Cornell three hours to live."

At Barton Hall the SDS rally had grown to over six thousand students and faculty. That evening the SDS apparently lost control of the meeting. They were recommending a building take-over that night. When news of the faculty meeting the next day was announced, the less radical group was willing to await that outcome. The atmosphere became much calmer. The moderates gained control of the group and they turned the meeting into a forum for constructive discussion.

Wednesday's faculty meeting again drew 1,100 members. These attendance figures are significant because routine faculty meetings had averaged fewer than three hundred members over recent years. The President, after making an opening statement, received a standing round of applause. Acting Dean Roberts moved for nullification of the judicial procedures taken against the blacks. After lengthy discussion, the faculty reversed its position of Monday and by a voice vote gave the motion a strong approval.

Many reasons have been advanced for the reversal of the position of the faculty. Concerned faculty had turned out for both meetings in large numbers, had learned more about the situation, and decided the blacks' case had merit. Others changed because they talked with many moderate students between the two meetings and found out that these concerned undergraduates, in large numbers, favored nullification. Other faculty took another look and changed because they felt that they must sacrifice principle to avoid violence and bloodshed on the campus and irreparable damage to the future of the University.

The above report of the six days is our attempt at an accurate chronicle of the important events of this period. It could not cover all points but we have tried to include the actions and events of significance.

ADDRESS IN BARTON HALL, APRIL 25, 1969

GEORGE MCT. KAHIN

George McT. Kahin was born in 1918. He is professor of government at Cornell, director of its Southeast Asia Program and Modern Indonesia Project. A frequent contributor to journals and publications dealing with Asian affairs, he is also the author of *Nationalism and Revolution in Indonesia* (Cornell University Press, 1952), and, together with John W. Lewis, *The United States in Vietnam* (Dial Press, 1967).

I come here as a man deeply worried over the sudden discovery of what I thought was impossible—amazed to find that something I have always taken for granted as a matter which all members of a university understood without question to be basic and absolutely essential to its functioning was not comprehended by large numbers of Cornell's students. I speak of that basic premise of a genuine university—academic freedom. Perhaps a generation which has never seen this challenged cannot be expected to be aware of it, or at least to perceive its absolute importance. But that quality in a university is something like breathing in the human body. You don't think about it; you take it for granted until suddenly you find yourself short of breath; once you begin to choke and gasp you suddenly are aware. But in the last few days I have to my consternation discovered that for much

of this student body this quality is either only dimly perceived or regarded as something very secondary to immediate
social objectives.

I have always disliked having to refer to personal experience. However, in view of the short time we have it is the
only way I know how to get this across to you. Some of
you, I think, know me as a rather severe critic of much of
our country's foreign policy. On these issues my judgments
are today apparently in harmony with a majority of you. Let
me assure you that it has not always been this way, and is a
recent phenomenon quite unrepresentative of my eighteen
years at Cornell. Indeed, these days I have sometimes felt
strange and very out of character. I am quite unused to having
a majority of this university community see American policies in Asia very much as I do.

When I first spoke and wrote against Vietnam policy the
majority of the students at this university were clearly against
me, some regarding me as unpatriotic and others as simply
lacking political virility. And it was very clear in the 1950s
when I was first at Cornell that most of my students felt
similarly opposed to my views concerning American foreign
policy. This was especially true in the McCarthy period,
when in the world outside the university so many of our
citizens found it expedient to discredit those they opposed
by smearing them with the charge of Communism. When I
came here to be interviewed for a job in 1951, I came as a
man already well smeared by McCarthyism. The department
chairman at the university I was leaving advised Cornell
that he suspected me of Communist views because I had
organized graduate students in defense of McCarthy's primary target, Owen Lattimore. I had no passport, that having
been lifted because the American Ambassador to Indonesia,
whose views I had strongly criticized, did not want me to
return to that country and also smeared me with the charge
of "Communist." I felt obliged, of course, to tell anyone
who contemplated hiring me about those charges. The chair-

man of the Department of Government was Herbert Briggs; the other three members were Robert Cushman, Mario Einaudi, and Clinton Rossiter. They hired me on the basis of what they regarded as my scholarly credentials. With respect to the McCarthyistic slander that I'd been smeared with, they acted in the terms of the maxim that a man is innocent until proven guilty, rather than the reverse of that maxim as then practiced by Joe McCarthy and by so much of American society outside of the university.

There were certainly pressures to conform projected from outside the university, and Joe McCarthy for a two-year period paid students or non-student informers to attend my classes and report everything I said. (They spoiled me for later generations of students, for never since have I had such reliable note-takers or any students who so hung on my every word.) But those pressures for conformity did not penetrate the walls of Cornell—walls, let me observe, whose outward side is strong, but which can be easily dismantled from inside. But my colleagues in the Department of Government, and in Cornell University, never so much as hinted that I should conform to the pressures from outside and refrain from speaking and writing as my conscience dictated.

For almost eighteen years now this university has given me a base, a sanctuary, a fortress from which I have been free to criticize as strongly as I wished whatever aspect of the Establishment's policies I chose, and I have chosen to be very strong in some of my criticism. During all these years I have had to deal with many pressures from outside the university, but never, not once, despite the frequent unpopularity of my views with large numbers of our students, have I ever felt from within the university any semblance whatsoever of pressure to desist from or curtail any object of inquiry, or alter what I believed I must say about my perceptions.

It is quite as imperative to me as a scholar that this freedom exist now as it was when so many students felt Joe McCarthy was an asset to our society, a man concerning whom they said they deplored his means but were willing to accept them in view of the ends he sought.

And with respect to McCarthyist tactics, let me assure you that calling a man a racist does not make him so, any more than McCarthy calling him a Communist made him a Communist. In their own way, and with genuine effect, my two departing colleagues, Walter Berns and Allen Sindler (and Clinton Rossiter as well), have fought against racism for a long time, beginning back when that fight was rather lonelier than it is today. If they are racists, then you may as well call me Walt W. Rostow.

These tactics continue. In this morning's *Sun,* I read that Mr. Thomas Jones accuses the Center for International Studies of being "deeply involved in developing counter-revolutionary tactics and anti-guerrilla tactics which are at this time being used primarily against colored people in the third world who are striving for their freedom, specifically the Vietcong." I would hope that Mr. Jones will have the good sense to retract such allegations because they are hideously false, and it is the height of social and moral irresponsibility for him to make those charges. It was the Center for International Studies and the Southeast Asia Program that spearheaded the fight against the Cornell Aeronautical Laboratory in Buffalo, which did sponsor counterinsurgency studies. We demanded that the laboratory be severed from the university, and it was. Mr. Jones is spreading a falsehood. I hope you will insist that he talk to someone who knows about the subject at hand before he makes other such preposterous allegations.

For me academic freedom has never previously seemed threatened at this university. But today I think it is. And it is primarily because of this, rather than any threats made over the radio, that my colleagues are leaving Cornell. You have asked us to understand why it was that the black students acted, to understand the fear they felt. It is fair that you ask this, and I'm sure a good many faculty and students did not sufficiently appreciate this before. But empathy must be two-sided if mutual understanding is to be achieved, and you too have an obligation to appreciate our views on the issue which we regard as every bit as crucial. What so many members of the Cornell faculty saw at stake in their meeting last Monday was, I can assure you, not the Cornell judicial system, nor was it the matter of justice for the blacks, something that most of those who voted as I did wanted as much as you. The issue that we saw as paramount was rather different. Remember you are dealing with a generation which went through the McCarthy period and whose minds were seared by it, just as your minds will for years to come be affected by the struggle for the blacks and a war in which so many of you want no part. We are keenly sensitized to issues of which I'm afraid you are still only partially aware. At Monday's meeting what so many members of the faculty saw before them was not a simple picture of a university official who felt obliged to sign an agreement against the background of firearms; the backdrop was hardly that simple. Because in the minds of most of us, behind men armed with guns (and for us it did not matter whether they were whites or blacks who held the guns)—behind them was the background of a very recent incident that cannot be washed away —the sordid spectacle of a colleague[1] physically pulled from a platform because he expressed views which some of his listeners didn't happen to like. That action was a direct assault on academic freedom. If it is to be condoned and excused as a political act, then academic freedom is in even greater jeopardy. It is that spectacle of force and intimidation and what it symbolizes that is uppermost in our minds, and which inevitably affected our perception of the relationship of guns to the agreements we were asked to endorse. We voted for the maintenance of academic freedom, believing that without that essential quality there can be no relationship of any kind between blacks and a university, because without

[1] President Perkins.—Eds.

that quality you don't have a university. The tragedy, I think, is that the university administration in communicating to you the results of the faculty vote on Monday did not convey this concern to you, didn't explain to you at all why we took the stand we did.

On Wednesday your faculty voted under what most of them perceived as continuing pressures of a threat of violence. Many of them have already told you why they voted differently on Wednesday than on Monday. It is essential you understand that. Like Professor Keeton and a number of others, I did so, but I didn't find it easy. As with him, I resented deeply having to act under the threat of violence, and that action cost me too some of my self-respect. Not simply because I was capitulating under force, but because I felt in doing so I was further undermining the foundations of academic freedom at Cornell. I voted differently on Wednesday because I discovered in talking to students on Tuesday and Wednesday morning that they had no realization that our Monday's stand was for academic freedom and against threats to compromise it, and that most of these students were completely confused by Secretary Roberts' statement[2] and assumed that Monday's vote had to do with the ends of the black students, rather than the means to be used in attaining them. If you had not perceived what was at stake it seemed to me absolutely incumbent that we gain enough time to explain to you what is at stake—that is, assuming you are interested in maintaining a university rather than destroying it. Most of us certainly were not voting against objectives of the black students. We were, let me repeat, voting against physical coercion on this campus—the use and threat of force which we perceived as a direct threat to academic freedom.

But there's more than this at stake, and I suppose that those students and faculty who regard themselves as revolutionaries are aware of this. If any of you do fancy yourselves

[2] A very snarled report of the faculty's action, broadcast on the campus radio.—Eds.

in the roles of revolutionaries, let me remind you that on this campus you are operating in a very special, protected, and permissive environment, one rather far removed from the brutal realities that govern the basic social conditions you say you want to change. Indeed, you operate in a context of freedom found in few other spots on this earth, one where the people you are trying to pressure are at a disadvantage, first because they happen to like you and share many of your values and objectives, and because as a consequence of their training and their own sense of values they are reluctant to meet force with force. Here on this campus where you are insulated from the hard and rough political factors that really dominate the over-all social environment—this is no testing ground for revolution. But it can be a testing ground for the political dialectic that force, once applied, is likely to beget a forceful reaction and a consequent escalation in the use of force. Those professors who are leaving this university recognize, as do I, that within a university efforts to achieve change through application of physical force are completely incompatible with the vital essence of university life, and will ultimately kill what you are trying to reform.

Once you accept that course for one group, no matter how urgent and praiseworthy their objectives, you open the door for those who oppose you to employ the same tactics; and if you are realistic rather than utopian you will know that outside the university there is a large portion of the society that is longing to crack down on the freedom of the universities, and which if you have sanctioned and blessed the use of force will use the same methods that you have found to be expedient short cuts to resolution of issues. And those forces can marshal immensely more power than you can. Do you really want to unleash them?

I intend to stay at Cornell University and do everything I can to maintain the principle that to me is essential to human progress—the freedom to think, speak, write, and advocate whatever a man honestly feels without the threat of physical force, whether under the cloak of political acts, political symbolism or whatever. But I use the word "university" advisedly—for unless that now terribly endangered principle of academic freedom remains operative here, we won't have a university.

PART I

Every generation imagines itself to be more intelligent than the one that went before it and wiser than the one that comes after it. This is an illusion and one should recognize it as such, but one also ought to stick to one's own world-view, even at the price of seeming old-fashioned: for that world-view springs out of experiences that the younger generation has not had, and to abandon it is to kill one's intellectual roots.

George Orwell

A PERSONAL NARRATIVE OF A RUDE AWAKENING

CUSHING STROUT

Cushing Strout was born in 1923. He is professor of English at Cornell, chairman of its Council for the Humanities, and a former member of its Commission for the Reform of Undergraduate Education (1965). He has published widely in the field of American intellectual history, including *The Pragmatic Revolt in American History: Carl Becker and Charles Beard* (Cornell Paperbacks Edition, 1966); *The American Image of the Old World* (Harper and Row, 1963); and is editor of *Hawthorne in England* (Cornell University Press, 1965); *Intellectual History in America* (Harper and Row, 1968); the John Harvard Library Edition of *The Spirit of American Government* (Belknap Press, 1965); and a case book on the Oppenheimer Hearings (Rand McNally, 1963).

> In like manner all public facts are to be individualized, all private facts are to be generalized.
>
> EMERSON

To a New Englander like myself, born on Patriots' Day, the nineteenth of April is memorable for "the shot heard round the world" at the Battle of Lexington and Concord. In 1969, on that same day in April, over fifty black militants at Cornell seized the student union, ousting many parents who had come for Parents Weekend. I remember thinking glumly that the date would not have sounded the same historical echo for the militant minority of black students, one sign of the depth of our racial crisis being the loss of a common political symbolism, a lack reflected in the demand on American campuses for separatist studies of black history and culture. In retrospect, it seems appropriate that on the day before the take-over of the building I had given a commentary at a historians' convention on a paper that emphasized the difficulties of writing traditional "general history" because of the pluralism of our intellectual and social life.

The sense of crisis was endemic. Grounded by bad weather in an airport lounge on my way back to Ithaca, after a long talk with a former student of mine embroiled in Harvard's troubles, I blurted out to a colleague and a graduate-student friend that I was sure Cornell would blow up before the term ended; therefore it would be necessary to try to organize "the middle" on our return. The prophecy was only a description. We came back to the exhausting round of meetings that are now part of nearly everyone's life in the no longer placid groves of academe. Only the summer's respite has given time to lift the moral burden of the past by writing about it, not as a recording angel but as a committed participant.

Events create their own past. I remember sitting in the faculty club, talking about the story of the Columbia crisis, *Up Against the Ivy Wall.* It seemed to me to illustrate a pathology of the university in which neither administration, faculty, nor students could act so as to prevent a deeply damaging result. "But it could never happen here," the same colleague remarked with his usual sanguine temper. I disagreed, but neither of us could have imagined then that we would in April watch two administrators trail along behind a column of black students emerging from the building with rifles and shotguns. He was actually only half wrong. What did happen was in some sense pathological and damaging, but it was certainly not the same story that the editors of the Columbia *Spectator* had told so well. Part of everyone's trouble, in fact, is the irresistible tendency to orient oneself in light of one's fearful images of what has happened at other universities, remaining blind to the peculiarities of one's own situation. The script is imagined in advance, roles are assigned, and the players learn their lines. But the production is partly another play. It calls desperately for an original reading, but it takes a determined effort of mind to respond to that call.

Campus issues are in one sense universal. The campus has become a surrogate for the world. All the passions generated by the world's agony are reanimated on campus with the peculiar intensity that symbolic questions inspire. The interminable, unjustified, misconceived war in Vietnam and the intractable, appalling injustices suffered by American black people are vivid on the backdrop of the stage. In the foreground: ROTC and the Black Studies Program. The world's evils have proved too recalcitrant to reform. The temptation is enormous to reduce them to manageable size in surrogate form. The price paid for that reduction is the turmoil that has given journalists new front-page copy.

Pundits have diagnosed the case: the university is complicit with the war, education is dominated by white middle-class standards, the academic departments are vested interests of guild conservatism. The young are fed up. It is all as true as any caricature. It may soon become established cant, for you can now hear in high places these echoes: "Knowledge is not an end in itself, nor is it a privilege to be hoarded by the privileged few." (Even Ben Franklin chided a utilitarian: "Of what use is a baby?") Or: we must not seek to "purge the university of contact with the real world and re-enter the sterility of a dead scholasticism." (The mind is not real? Who is proposing scholasticism?) Or: ". . . is it not better to make the effort to understand rather than to secure a solution by force?" (Better as a response to force itself?) Or: "the university will either share in the life and the turmoil of our revolutionary world, or it will be a morgue."

(But it has its own terms for such sharing and turmoil tends to debase them.)

I am quoting from the final speech of President Perkins on Commencement Day. It received a short standing ovation, from convention, from respect for the gracefully departing, but surely also from pleasure in the liberal sentiments. The American taste for liberal rhetoric on ceremonial occasions is notorious. It is what people come to hear—parents in their respectable clothes, students in their dignified gowns, the lawns a stunning green, a lilt in the music, and the "turmoil of our revolutionary world" briefly submerged in everybody's thoughts.

The President could speak with satisfaction, however, because there was the elected Constituent Assembly of some four hundred people, engaged for the summer in "restructuring" the university. There was the recent announcement that a black director of Cornell's new Black Studies Program had been found. There had been no police "bust," only some property damage, a few muggings, and the campus looked stunning on Commencement. In the President's sanguine view "Cornell . . . was a remarkably steady ship in the storm, . . . it held its course . . . once more in calm seas we will all be proud to have helped Cornell through." Only one sentence disturbed this glowing account: black students "will also have to summon their innate practical sense not to push their militancy so far that it polarizes the faculty, paralyzes the administration, turns away their friends, and ultimately imperils the educational opportunity itself." (The tense of the verb appeared to suggest that the calamity had not yet happened.) Fairness requires mention of another presidential phrase, pointing to darker knowledge gained from any crisis: "few of us can be wholly pleased with the truths we discover about ourselves." It is those truths about Cornell collectively that it would be important to hear about, however unsuitable they might have been for the gay occasion of Commencement Day in the kind of weather that Ithaca saves

for special occasions, like the sudden loveliness of a change-
able woman, dressing up for company.

Nobody can speak definitively for black people. But the
isolation of Ithaca must be a dubious experience for those
black students, pulled out of the ghettos and rural South on
the basis of deliberately lowered academic standards, to participate in the President's experiment of Cornell's four-year-
old Special Educational Project (COSEP), first suggested by
a physicist. Without much connection to a very small downtown constituency of black citizenry, in a university with
virtually no black faculty, black students must be under pressure to demonstrate their militancy in compensation for their
distance from "where the action is." For the administration,
the program of black studies was, in any case, negotiated under pressure behind the scenes on the theory that it was
"what the blacks want," though what they wanted was a
function of what faction happened at different times to be
dominant in the Afro-American Society. The actual diversity
of the black liberation movement was thus simplified to the
insistent pressure of a local caucus.

Black student leaders had met at Howard University on
Thanksgiving, 1968. Cornell had previously moved to establish an academically oriented black studies program involving white professors,[1] but in December forty black students stridently proclaimed themselves the new committee,
seized a building (scheduled to be given them later) for
themselves, and a week afterwards disruptively demonstrated
on the campus with toy pistols, African dancing on the student union's dining tables, and the dumping of piles of books
from the library's shelves onto the circulation desk because
of their "irrelevance." In negotiations with the students demanding "autonomy" for a Black College there was ghetto-
language verbal abuse by some blacks, and one carried a
boldly displayed knife in his boot. In January the Afro-

[1] The committee included eight students and nine faculty, many
of them radical-activist in sympathy.

American Society proposed a candidate for director of a Black Studies Center, a twenty-nine-year-old graduate student who had a brilliant college record and had led a sit-in at his own university. The administration began negotiations with him almost immediately, though he himself delayed final acceptance until early June. In early March seven black students proposed that for non-tenure appointments a small outside panel of black experts, selected by two administrators, the director, and three black students, have the final decision in case of any disagreement between the director and the administrators over a candidate. (For tenure appointments Cornell faculty would be involved in the ratio of two to three from the outside panel.) The administration accepted this leaky, unprecedented arrangement unknown to the faculty at large. By April the trustees had budgeted $240,000 for the Center.

In the President's view the March arrangement was, no doubt, one of those examples of how a white university should take up the responsibility of educating black students by making, as he remarked in his Commencement speech, "the adjustments necessary to insure its success." And he added: "Unfortunately, we have not all learned to make the adjustments—we, the white majority; we, the architects of separatism; we, the standard-makers." Just what sort of success would be insured by this hugger-mugger way of developing black studies he did not explain. The predictable effect was to surround the Center with suspicion, fear, and mistrust, a dubious service to young blacks who had a valid claim on a serious program.

I believe (as I once wrote the student newspaper) that not only are black studies capable of making a contribution to both history and literature, but that a professor for valid pedagogical reasons might want to divide his course into black and white sections—a division that most people I talked with found invidious, as if it were the same thing as a dominant group imposing racial segregation on an op-

pressed group. Certainly the black students had been forced
to contend at Cornell with the traditional liberal argument
that one should *always* be "color blind," as if skin color was
only a natural and not a historical fact, embedded in the
social experience and emerging identities of millions of people.
But the traditionalists, however trite their arguments or however conservative their view of their fields, were at least right
in suspecting that the movement for black studies at Cornell
was taking an aggressively political direction without any
administrative public statement of academic guidelines or
faculty involvement in its development.[2]

On the day that the blacks took the Straight they would
broadcast on the student radio station that they had seized
the building because of the university's "racist attitudes" and
because it "lacked a program relevant to the black students."
By any fair accounting the university had in fact moved with
remarkable if undignified and secretive haste to "give the
blacks what they wanted," short of the "autonomy" that was
legally impossible under university charter without state legislative action.

The early spring of 1969 was also disturbed by another
crisis of special interest to humanities professors, who felt
little confidence in the administration's willingness to support
strong programs in their area. Their traditions and innova-
tions are more congenial to that fading image of a durable,
independent, and elegant "ivory tower," scorned by both
radicals and philistines. In March, as chairman of the Humanities Council, I wrote for the student paper an article on
the critical problems of the humanities at Cornell. Many
valuable professors had chosen to leave Cornell, and most

---

[2] A tentative syllabus of black studies once proposed by some
students for fall, 1969, included among twenty-six courses "Studies
in the Strategy of Confrontation" and "Theory and Practice in the
Use of Small Arms and Hand to Hand Combat." (Document sent
to me through the courtesy of Theodore Draper and Clinton
Rossiter.)

humanists felt that the administration exposed its tin ear whenever it spoke, as it seldom did, about the humanities. "In a time when the drift of events nationally is marked by 'non-negotiable demands' and 'other-directed' responses to them," I wrote, "the future threatens to become the haphazard equilibrium of mounting pressures from those who have the power to make the most trouble." Militant students, it was clear, would have more muscle than professors. The conflicts that they posed, I felt, would not "permit us to look like men who are always on the side of the angels, particularly when there are no angels." Unfortunately, some liberals are as concerned about their "image" as some administrators are. Gentle, sensitive people, with a real concern for social justice and some ambivalence about the value of academic intellectual work, were also increasingly becoming apologists for a local black caucus that was steadily taking on a paramilitary style of public address.

April is the cruelest month. In retrospect, the pattern of responding to aggressive action by accommodation had begun a year ago, in April 1968, when fifty blacks forcibly occupied the office of the chairman of economics for six hours in protest against the allegedly covert racism of a visiting professor. His pedagogy may have been rather stiff, but the demand for his dismissal threatened academic freedom. The event coincided with the national tragedy of the murder of Martin Luther King, Jr. There were fires in Ithaca, and I remember calling my wife from Wesleyan University, where I was giving a paper, to check nervously on local conditions. On my return we attended a memorial service downtown and were more shocked by the national disaster than by confused reports about what had happened in our backyard. (In the 1950s right-wing students had hissed my lectures at Yale and complained to the chairman, but I did not see the parallel until much later.) No one was charged, and the dean circulated a disturbing memo that exonerated individuals but accepted the doctrine of Cornell's complicity with all whites in a "covert racism" of ignorance and indifference.

The President's Special Commission on the affair of the visiting professor (Michael McPhelin) spoke confidently enough in general terms: "the right to be mistaken is essential for free inquiry"; "the professor obviously must have the authority to maintain essential orderliness in his class"; "Cornell University neither supports nor sanctions violence on the part of complaining members of the academic community." But when it came to the difficult particulars, its voice faltered. Emphasizing the factors of poor advice and information, "constricted and unsatisfactory communication," and "mutual lack of understanding," it faulted the chairman of the Department of Economics because he "unfortunately did not respond to the depth and seriousness of the students' feelings, choosing instead to discuss questions of academic freedom."

Cornell, the Commission said, is "a microcosm of the world in which we live," but in that world black power advocates were mounting confrontations "to heighten the contradictions," acting out their image of themselves as a colonial people in an imperialist mother country. (In retrospect it seems no accident that McPhelin, a Jesuit who had recently lived in the Philippines, would be a suitable target.) Whatever the extent of the professor's "covert racism" (for which evidence is very meager), it was being measured not by ordinary standards of prejudice but by active members of a militant political organization dedicated to a tendentious theory of black culture. It was the influence of this ideology that led three members of the Commission itself to complain against a widely used textbook's statement ("close and continuous contact has given Caucasoids and Negroids the same basic western European type of culture") on the non-scientific political ground that it "denigrates the present interest of black people in their own culture and development," an emphasis "vital" to their "well-being."

The President's definition of the Special Commission's goals had heavily tipped the balance at the outset in the students' favor by neglecting to mention any issue of academic freedom. Instead he asked the Commission to determine if the university had adequate procedures "for considering and acting on complaints of the character made by the Afro-American Society," to consider the advisability of a larger inquiry into "racial bias in teaching" or the curriculum, and to recommend improvements regarding "any problems related to race in the university." Despite this one-sided charge, the Commission made two long-range proposals that went well beyond the President's understanding of the problem: a campaign by administrators and faculty to inform the community "on an urgent, continuing basis" of the principles and procedures of academic freedom and the future development of Black Studies in the light of "full communication" between the central administration, the faculty, and student groups. It was ominous for the future of Cornell that these critical proposals fell on deaf ears until the severe crisis of the following April harshly demonstrated their importance.

Meanwhile the unfortunate Professor McPhelin, who had agreed—*before* the demand for his dismissal was made—to apologize to his large lecture class for precipitating the trouble by ignoring a black student's challenging question, quietly gave up his scheduled lecture on poverty because he was advised to "stay off it." Surely if he had been a left-wing economist, who had irritated some reactionary organization of white students, the prevalent campus image of the affair would have been very different. While the academic principles involved would not have changed, somebody else's political ox would have been gored.

Liberal guilt feelings were widespread on the campus, and they would later be exploited during the turmoil of the crisis engendered by the take-over of Willard Straight Hall. In that context the charge of "institutional racism" would become as non-empirical as original sin and just as effective in con-

verting souls to the preachers' radical political revivalism.
Faculty had displayed its vulnerability in the Educational
Policy Committee's turnabout, criticizing a proposed student-
run SDS course on revolution while some weeks later giving
credit, with two dissents, to a course on radical black ideology
taught by a SNCC field organizer who had never completed
college.

The "blowup" finally came over the campus judiciary system. By April 22, at the height of campus tension, a student
leader of the Afro-American Society, addressing thousands
of students in Barton Hall, could say: "Now the pigs are
going to die too. When people like J.P. . . . are going to be
dealt with. . . . We are moving tonight. Cornell has until
nine to live." By a 3–1 show of hands a crowd of six thousand
would vote to support black demands that the faculty rescind
the student-faculty Conduct Board's decision to "reprimand"
three blacks who had demonstrated in December with toy
guns. (History was in an ironic mood: the leader, a freshman
class president and an author of the judicial system itself,
would have been head of the Conduct Board that tried the
cases if he had not resigned the year before. One SDS leader
was an approving member of the report that led to the
campus judiciary system.) On March 12 this collision course
had been set when the university faculty voted that the
charged black students were obliged to appear before the
board, as they had previously refused to do.

The context of the faculty's vote was decisive. In late
February, SDS and AAS members had angrily confronted
the President, at a symposium on South Africa, and challenged the university's investments in South Africa, made
indirectly through the Chase Manhattan Bank. (It later turned
out that the investments had been already routinely sold.)
Two blacks with clubs dominated the stage; one of them
was a former student who had roughed up a reporter for the
student newspaper in December; the other grabbed the President by the collar in anger at his account of university policy.

(Cited by the Board, the student dropped out of Cornell.) The President silently left the auditorium, while a visiting South African black condemned the assault. In early March, members of SDS and the AAS broke into Malott Hall and forced cancellation of a recruiting visit by representatives from Chase Manhattan Bank. No one was charged or punished. Students assumed that politically motivated actions were above campus law. It was this pattern of repeated intimidation, without articulate or firm administrative response, that deeply worried many faculty members at the March 12 meeting.

From a political point of view the December cases before the faculty were less than ideal. They involved incidents that had not been seriously disruptive, though they had included symbolic weapons and stolen furniture. Most of us were not clear just which events were involved, for nothing was said about them at the meeting.[3] Also there were no black students on the Board; however, only three out of nearly one hundred voluntary applicants for participation in the judicial system had been black. These limitations did not seem fatal to me; furthermore, the Provost had told me before the meeting that the mood of the blacks was more cooperative than it had been and that they had agreed to appear before the Board.

To many, including myself, what was at issue was an alarming tendency on the part of a large minority in the faculty to vote ritualistically for general principles in support of a campus judiciary system and of non-disruptive means of persuasion, provided they did not have any actual application to any concrete cases, especially if they involved black

[3] I learned much later that the Board understood from discussions with the AAS that it did not *then* consider the cited incidents as group-sanctioned political acts. The AAS changed its position later. A visiting radical black writer, Michael Thelwell, described the toy-gun demonstrators as acting "obviously on some revolutionary fantasy of their own." *Ramparts 8* (July 1969), 51.

students. The tendency of faculties to endorse glittering generalities without making anyone, including themselves, pay for them is one of the corrupting features of academic life. The majority, however, voted that "refusal to accept the jurisdiction of the adjudicatory system through deliberate refusal to appear before the appropriate board or through deliberate refusal to comply with its sanctions is an implicit denial of membership in the educational community. Such refusal cannot help but expose the student to the imposition of serious penalties." The Provost, appearing more as a member of the faculty than as an administrator, spoke of the meeting as a time of crisis in which a pattern of confrontation was increasingly evident in Cornell's life, and the majority had responded to his somber tone by its vote, a narrow 57%.

To the black students the vote was anticipated as "a challenge to black people's right to organize and act politically" and taken as "a test of our unity, solidarity, and seriousness." They interpreted the Board's action as "selective reprisal" and a "backlash" response to their demand for a black studies program. The Afro-American Society, instead of the charged blacks, therefore appeared before the Board in a body, announcing that whenever the "necessities of black people come into conflict with established forms and procedures" it would be "absurd and unjust to expect that the university or its agencies can adjudicate such matters since they are in fact party to the action." They suggested the model of outside arbitration as in labor-management disputes. Many faculty liberals heaved a sigh of relief that the blacks' tone was "reasonable" and closed their eyes to what they had, in fact, said.

The notion of the university as only a faction in a struggle for power was a rude challenge to the traditional idea of an academic community, capable of keeping its own house in order apart from state intervention. It seemed to me that empathy for blacks did not displace the need for judgment and that the political power of the Afro-American Society

was as much a reality as the "black needs" that influenced so
many people's reading of the situation. The Conduct Board
withdrew its suspension-judgment and asked for guidance
from a Faculty Committee on Student Affairs. On March 16
three whites were beaten up on campus. Two identified their
assailants only as being black; the third, who was nearly
murdered, never knew what had hit him. It was a bad spring
all over the country. I was very disturbed at the Orwellian
ring of the description of a black rebel at San Francisco
State, whose bomb had exploded in his hands, as "an innocent
victim of white oppression," and a liberal white advocate of
its black studies program was called "a fascist pig" for a
critical article he had written about it. It might happen here
—especially if we only imagined that Columbia could happen
here.

History went on a lark again. The Faculty Committee on
Student Affairs, led by the chairman of the department of
government, backed the judiciary system and the Conduct
Board in a detailed rational response to the Afro-American
Society's polemical position. In mid-April, however, the Faculty Council revealed a hitherto strangely unmentioned fact,
that the Student Conduct Board's summons, sent to defendants, also said: "If you fail to appear at a hearing or to
cooperate in a reasonable manner, the Board may proceed
to judgment." The statement was interpreted as meaning that
no defendant need appear and therefore could not be suspended for non-appearance. It tended to becloud the status
of the system itself with a fog of ambiguity. The Afro-
American Society harshly denounced the Faculty Committee
on Student Affairs (FCSA). Ironically, it rejected "liberal
'sympathy and sensitivity'" and asked for "Justice," while
the Society's defenders continued to plead for the sympathy
and sensitivity that the blacks rejected. The student newspaper grasped desperately at the solution of judging the
blacks *in absentia* with light penalties that could be "ignored
by everyone" so that discussion of a new and better judicial

system could begin. The FCSA took the hint and so instructed the Conduct Board. For the blacks, however, accepting the judicial system was like accepting the tax on the tea that was thrown into Boston Harbor. It challenged their separatism.

At this point history escalated into the sequence of events that put the pictures of armed black students, emerging in Che Guevara poses from the student union after thirty-four hours of occupation, on front pages all over the country: a series of false fire alarms in the early hours of Friday morning, April 18, the Conduct Board's sentence of mild reprimands to three black students for "harassment and intimidation," and—an hour later—the appalling discovery of a flaming cross on the front porch of the black girls' dorm.[4] At dawn of the next day a minority of the black students, many of them girls, took over Willard Straight Hall, supported by an SDS picket line. About ten fraternity boys foolishly broke through a window and, ejected after a scuffle, muttered about mobilizing and "cleaning the place out." That night, probably in a mixed mood of fear and bravado, the black students began to smuggle their rifles and ammunition into the building.

Fantasies of white reprisals were used to justify the introduction of weapons into the Straight, and many whites were eager to believe them in order to keep intact their own image of the weak and victimized blacks. (Later, a small investigating committee, including one black professor and a young left-wing teacher, was unable to find any substance to the Afro-American Society's charge of complicity between the campus police and the fraternity boys, or any factual basis for the Mississippi-like rumors of armed white avengers.) Some of the militants boasted in the same breath of their

[4] The cross became a powerful point in various apologies for the take-over, but some months later the most vocal militant during the crisis publicly admitted that plans had been made earlier, that the occupation was not done "on the spur of the moment."

"non-violent" behavior and of their pride in taking a revolutionary posture that had "galvanized black people across this nation."

The curtain on this melodrama went up slowly for me. News of the take-over came over the car radio as we drove into Ithaca on a wintry Saturday, returning from the convention in Philadelphia, but the guns had not yet been introduced into the plot. My wife and I went to a "teach-in" where the SDS faculty adviser sentimentally spoke to enthusiastic applause about the "powerlessness" of the blacks at Cornell. It *had* happened here but in a new context of permissive paternalism.

On Sunday the round of anxious telephone calls began, plunging the campus into the atmosphere of continuous crisis. My colleagues and I watched the black students march from the Straight, their guns held in guerrilla style, their exit cheered with clenched fists (and clenched minds) by the SDS. We followed the blacks to their headquarters, which they guarded like a fort while two administrators signed the evacuation agreement that included the Dean of the Faculty's private pledge to urge the faculty to rescind the reprimands or accept his own resignation. There had been no police cordon of the Straight, no previous preparations for an injunction procedure (even the Interfraternity Council was persuaded to oppose it), and blacks had been allowed to come and go from the Straight as they pleased, a policy based on a desire to avoid the scuffle that had taken place during the occupation of the economics office a year before. Much later I would learn that a reliable dorm counselor had even told one vice president on Saturday morning that she had just seen a black leader calling out to the blacks in the Straight to go get their guns.[5] Fear of Harvard's "bust" had paralyzed Cornell.

[5] Taped interview with the counselor by Dr. Howard Feinstein. For the failure to prepare for an injunction see *The Report of the Special Trustee Committee on Campus Unrest at Cornell* (September 5, 1969), p. 28.

Meeting with a hastily improvised group of professors, including a few supporters and friends of the President, I helped draft motions for the faculty meeting: condemning the cross-burning as "a despicable attack," refusing to accept the rescinding of the reprimands (without regard to their merit) under the conditions of extortion that had been allegedly required to get the armed students out of the building, proposing expulsion for the carrying of arms in demonstrations or counterdemonstrations thereafter, and offering to work with the Afro-American Society in developing a judicial system that all our students would consider fair. Our options were drastically reduced by the situation that the administration had allowed to develop. Some older members of our caucus alerted the President, and I was delegated to present the motions to the faculty on the following day. As we began to break up in exhaustion, I asked anxiously: "Are we prepared to will the consequences?" I was answered: "We'll face them when we come to them." Sufficient unto the day . . .

Our motions engendered a confused four-hour debate in the largest faculty meeting ever held at Cornell. By then the President, in touch with trustees, the mayor, and state and local police, had declared an "emergency" and threatened suspension for any student carrying a gun on campus or engaging in a coercive occupation of a building. Any organization promoting such occupation would be disbanded. The horse having gone, the barn door was to be locked. At the meeting he stepped into the faculty deadlock to offer his own seven-point motion, written in pencil on the back of an envelope. It entirely ignored the cross incident, promised a review of the Afro-American Society's political complaints "under secure and non-pressurized circumstances," and left the reprimands on record for the time being because of "the presence of arms and the seizure of the Straight." It also contained a characteristically patronizing expression of "sympathy for the problems of the black students in adjusting themselves to life at Cornell," which the blacks would later scorn.

Dispersed, our caucus lost communication with itself, and under pressure some began to grasp publicly at the solution offered by the President, who was trying to define a milder consensus as well as garner support for his recent "emergency" declaration. I tried to pick out on the President's envelope those statements I thought consistent with our group's motions. I deliberately exempted the patronizing clause, but reluctantly agreed to accept the others. It was too late for distinctions. A tired and hungry faculty, we voted (726–281) for the seven points, and at the last moment someone had the sense to add the neglected condemnation of the cross-burning. As we left the meeting, I was troubled by the confusion we had experienced. Already in the caucus there were evident signs of conflict, and it had taken the faculty four hours to come to a conclusion, formulated by the President himself. The faculty was an ungainly actor in a crisis.

On Tuesday we faced the consequences we had not calculated earlier. And it also became clear how frail the padlock was that the President had put on the barn door. I was invited by a friend to a meeting of the left "Concerned Faculty" to hear the black leaders, and was dismayed to see twenty-six of my colleagues, some in my own department, a few my friends, vote to take a building in sympathy with the blacks. There were then hundreds of state police and local sheriffs on the outskirts of the campus, and the blacks still had their guns somewhere. One of the black leaders personally proposed a "shoot-out" with the "pigs" if they sought to prevent another black seizure that surely would be made if the faculty did not reverse itself. SDS, shamed by the blacks' audacity, was burning to take its own building. One black leader scored the faculty for its ignorant description of the cross-burning as a "childish prank," a confusion, in fact, with what the President had earlier said. I asked to speak to correct him but was voted down. Instead I wrote a letter on the spot and gave it to him, explaining that we had called it a "despicable attack" and urging him not to "paint the faculty into a corner."

By the end of the day there was a tide of sentiment in favor of rescinding the reprimands because the circumstances were both dangerously combustible in terms of armed conflict and politically untenable in the light of the thousands of students sitting in at Barton Hall under SDS leadership and in sympathy with the blacks. The unorganized student "middle" was very effective in curbing the SDS vanguard's wish to take disruptive action; the price that moderates willingly paid was the rescinding of the reprimands, penalties that did not seem just to them. As various colleges, sometimes in faculty meetings invaded by students (as ours was), began to vote heavily in favor of rescinding, a professor of government sympathetic to the "Concerned Faculty" successfully urged "rational radicals" at Barton Hall not to act impulsively but to await the results of the next day's faculty decision. His remarks and the votes shifted the balance and turned the occupation into a festive all-night "sit-in," which the President then defined as legal, giving the black leaders an opportunity to cite this reversal of his own position as an illustration of "institutional racism."

For most faculty and many students not caught up in mob psychology, there was for many days a felt vacuum of leadership in the university, a void filled by the plebiscite that came to be called "the Body" at Barton Hall. The President, speaking before some nine thousand students and faculty on Monday, had incredibly said nothing about the actual situation and delivered himself instead of "enlightened" platitudes that led some to suspect that he had in fact given his speech on "The Prospects for Stability" that the occupation of the Straight had forced him to cancel, the "prospects" at that point having been none too good. This crashing failure looked even worse when some of us discovered later that he had privately told a professor in our caucus that blacks had threatened on the telephone to take over the microphone to give their own view if he *did* address himself to the actual situation. We were stunned on that critical Tuesday evening to hear a radio address by a black leader who totally unjustifiably singled out several faculty and administrators by name as "racists" to be "dealt with" by the Afro-American Society. (Some of those named moved their families into motels.) One of my advisees, who had criticized the drift of events as a student editor, was frightened enough by a threatening phone call to ask for refuge in my house. One black student, menaced by militants, fled to Canada.

A smog of bellicose rhetoric hung over the campus. When the university faculty, in a foregone conclusion, voted for the motion of our caucus[6] to rescind the reprimands on Wednesday, the leaders of the Barton Hall crowd were arrogantly and menacingly jubilant: "That decision," the Afro-American Society spokesman asserted, "was made right here. They didn't make any decision; they were told from this room what to do." It was a bitter potion to add to the crow already eaten by the faculty in an untenable political situation in order to avoid a bloody battleground. Some professors, who had reversed their position, convinced themselves in public that it was a matter of reason. For those of us who felt that it was a "reason" made necessary by the scale of the pending threats, the possibly itchy trigger fingers of the local deputies, and the emotional fervor of the majority of students, the reversal had a bad taste. I went into the almost deserted student coffee shop to wash it down with a cup of tea, taken with two very quiet colleagues. Meanwhile (I learned later) the President, who had taken much of the faculty with him from Bailey to Barton Hall, received a vote of confidence from the students and was kept waiting on the

[6] At the last minute one of the professors who had been attacked on the radio as a "racist" asked if he could present the motion and did so.

floor while a black leader mocked "the fatherly arm" that had been put on his shoulder, and an SDS leader brazenly swigged from the President's Pepsi-Cola can. Then all hands went up in victory for what the President called "one of the most constructive, positive forces ever set in motion in the history of Cornell": the mass meeting of students.

Defeat was to be dubbed victory through "restructuring." The President had improvised a very small committee of students and professors, resulting in a vague, last-minute motion in the meeting at Bailey Hall to devise "a broadly based body" to recommend "our future courses of action." It had passed almost unanimously without debate in the wake of the vote rescinding the reprimands. Some of my students and their friends came to my house and told me that the Body at Barton Hall was "restructuring" the university by a show of hands. I reminded them of *The Federalist:* "Had every Athenian citizen been a Socrates, every Athenian Assembly would still have been a mob."

For the rest of the week "the Barton and Bailey Circus" was marked by an extraordinary self-flagellation for "racism," including sinners who came to the anxious bench to announce their conversion in public confession. It was a political Great Awakening with the radical leaders playing the role of Jonathan Edwards. One student perceptively wrote to the student newspaper about his feelings as part of the crowd: "I knew . . . that I should conquer that bigotry and resentment within my institutionalized soul and be willing to go out and destroy and kill or be destroyed and be killed with the Afro-Americans. This I could not do, but I could sit and listen. . . . The SDS leader convinced us, a curious and concerned audience, that we had seized Barton Hall and done something beautiful, when WE had done nothing at all. In fact we had become mere voyeurs and prostitutes, leaving behind an ambiguous act to be exploited by those who had seduced us."

The "victory" celebration had a high bill that soon came

due—the resignation from the university of three very much respected professors.[7] Two of them had been smeared as "racists" by the black demagogue on Tuesday: the major architect of the judicial system and the recent winner of a teaching award. Professors of government, they became convinced, in anger and despair, that the administration had conspired to use student power to humble faculty power at the accepted expense of academic freedom—beginning in April 1968. Over twenty professors told the President they would cease teaching until all firearms had been removed from all students. (Some fraternities turned in their guns, and the blacks dispersed their weapons somewhere off campus.) In history and government many, on this legally impractical condition, gave up formal teaching for the term. It was left to a young visiting professor to respond more effectively by organizing a faculty "teach-in" in Barton Hall on the issue of academic freedom, a theme most persuasively developed by Professor George McT. Kahin.

Many of us believed that boycotting classes in the crisis was not a defense of free speech, which is seldom maintained by silence; and for me the classroom was a lifeline to reality at a time when the public dialogue had become infected with ideology, a corruption of ideas. My own students, both freshmen and upperclassmen, nevertheless were for the most part still very much open to critical inquiry and response; and by the following week they were even eager to return to discussion of the material, rather than of Cornell. (It was a happy stroke of fortune that for the rest of the term I was teaching Lionel Trilling's *The Middle of the Journey,* Hemingway's *For Whom the Bell Tolls,* Ralph Ellison's *Invisible Man,* and David Riesman's *The Lonely Crowd.* By accident my teaching was "relevant" to the crisis in the mediated way that serves a teacher best.)

[7] Another resigned from the chairmanship of the History Department and received the support of 225 history students who requested the resignation of the President without prejudice to "the legitimate needs of the Afro-American Society."

Shortly after the "teach-in" on academic freedom I helped organize a declaration of forty-one professors, assuring our students that we would stay in touch with them and implicitly warning the administration that, if the conditions for maintaining academic freedom and scholarly standards degenerated further, we would act together, and the time might be "dangerously near." A few signers had been "established" administration supporters, many more were not. We agreed that the present moment was not the time to urge the President's resignation or our own.

The Barton Hall "Body" posed the danger, as some of us saw it, that certain necessary functions of the faculty would be treated as only another factional interest to be thrown into the boiling stew of "restructuring." To guard against this danger I joined with some physicists to prepare and defend a motion to have a committee of professors delineate the necessary duties of the faculty in preserving standards. (It passed unanimously only because it was separated from the vote on the Constituent Assembly, and it was not acted on until the following academic year.) This fear was not necessarily a conservative one. I had worked for over a month as chairman of a student-faculty committee to revise the graduate field of English, grown rigid and conventional in its requirements in contrast to the general freedom of the Cornell special-committee system. With younger colleagues I had invited an SDS student to make his critique of the program for the students and the faculty long before the crisis. The concern that he stirred up was, I believe, fruitful and necessary to bring about changes over which the department itself was closely divided. The general crisis made it possible later for that revisionary report to be largely approved by the department, though my educational allies were not my political ones.

In the first flush of the "restructuring" fever my large department had met commune-style in a student-faculty plenum. I entered it to find a student in the chair, the majority voting to meet every day until the end of term. There was a fog of talk about "racism." This "participatory democracy" with a vengeance I boycotted most of the time, except to argue that it was necessary for the sake of mutual respect to make it clear that the faculty has legitimate interests and academic values to assert and defend. SDS graduate students spoke of "power" as if it were a numinous object that somebody was meanly squandering and refusing to share with them. That there are student and faculty interests that often, but not always, overlap is, in Madisonian terms, the common sense of the matter. It was, however, a long time before common sense was common at Cornell that spring. To speak truth to power, in the old Quaker phrase, should have a new bearing to include "black power" or "student power." But when the campus has become a surrogate for the world, the facts are concealed by the persistent image of power as something that only the "Establishment" holds, even if during one week it has visibly collapsed before one's eyes.

Old forms persist and reassert themselves. The student revolution is too much of a mood, temporarily congealed around an issue, to make deeply radical changes. There is, in fact, a danger that "restructuring" will fail entirely to deal with the *intellectual* revision of academic business, traditionally tied to the departmental model. The thrust of "student power" at Cornell was to perpetuate that model in new form merely by enlarging it for a while to include undergraduates and graduates in plenary sessions. From the point of view of those working for some more flexible interdisciplinary grouping of professors, the "revolution" was not innovative but dogmatically democratic in a simplistic form. It envisaged, as the President explained to the faculty, an end to the functional separation of powers in academic life—a community in which all the parts were "concerned with all matters."

If there was ever any risk that the university would become some rarefied feast of reason on a mountaintop, the "revolution" proved the fear ludicrous. Its style was far more congenial to indoctrination than to critical inquiry. The black studies program itself will necessarily deal with ideology, but that it will draw strength from the diversity of the black liberation movement and from the possibilities of critical exploration of its meaning is much in doubt.[8] One of the director's first choices for faculty in the Africana Center was an unsuccessful student in philosophy, chiefly notorious for his demagogic attacks on Jewish schoolteachers in New York. Against this backdrop, darkened further by three days of muggings by blacks on campus, including a hold-up, our "Committee of 41" discovered what the March appointment procedures for the Center actually were,[9] and I reported to the administration that we thought them entirely inadequate. The President's rationalizing response was to agree with us as readily as if the procedures had been set up behind his back. By then the administration had consulted some Cornell faculty on the controversial candidate, thus burning its fingers on its own procedure. It reverted to an earlier plan with more administrative control and vetoed the candidate. Faculty in general characteristically were not told in detail about this history until just before Commencement.

The Barton Hall student "task force on racism" and some of the "left" faculty began to rouse fears about "reactionary" professors "sabotaging" the black studies program. Unable to agree sufficiently to back any public statement, whose impact many members feared, our group was thus given whatever political identity other groups found it useful to

[8] It should be said, however, that the Educational Policy Committee of the College of Arts and Sciences passed for academic credit all ten of the courses submitted by the Africana Center in the fall of 1969. My doubts had been accentuated in the crisis by the incoming Director's preference for the programs at Federal City College and Merritt College, then in turmoil, rather than Yale's. In a recent public statement he stressed, however, that black studies "must emphasize rigorous scholarship."

[9] An incomplete version of them was published in the student newspaper only eight days before the take-over.

impute to it. Effective political action, I concluded, could not
be based on professors, who are used to holding on to every
shred of their individual sovereignty, rather like Southern
states. As the President began to talk of seeing us all in the
fall, while circulating to chairmen admiring letters from
alumni and wealthy donors, the campus continued to split
over his stewardship. I felt it would be necessary to tell a
trustees' investigating group that there was a crisis of confidence in the administration's leadership. A caucus of about
twenty agonizingly agreed so to act, but without explicitly
calling for any resignations. In the end the group came un-
raveled in an unwillingness to make any further public statement—even about its demise. Humanists and scientists in
our caucus tended to feel differently about an administration
that had to its credit significant accomplishments in the
building up of a Division of Biology. The President con-
fessed, however, that an open letter from a group of law
professors, some of them his friends, who felt he had not
given academic freedom first priority, most influenced his
decision to resign.

Clio at Cornell showed a taste for symbolism in the style
of the theater of the absurd. A mild censure for brandishing
toy pistols had led to the brandishing of real rifles. By their
own attacks on the campus judiciary system, contemptuously
dismissed as "Mickey Mouse," the radical students paved
the way for their own treatment at the hands of civil authority. Before the crisis some SDS members had constructively
induced the university into negotiations with the town to
improve provision of low-income housing. After the crisis a
small group of SDS members, who harmlessly protested
against an ROTC ceremony by painting a cannon in a restricted section of Barton Hall, were turned over to civil
authority for a misdemeanor that the campus judiciary would
have treated more appropriately. To add the final touch of
the ludicrous, woven like a ragged thread through the whole
semester at Cornell, it turned out that the cannon was not

government property after all; it had been sold as scrap to a local company in April. The administration had granted amnesty to the black students, but a grand jury charged them with criminal trespass. The predictable effect of the photographs of armed students was a legislative demand from Albany for a tighter system of regulatory measures on college campuses.

The Port Huron Statement of SDS (1962) nobly affirmed a belief in "power and uniqueness rooted in love, reflectiveness, reason and creativity." What I remember most painfully about Cornell that spring of 1969 was the noisy absence of those virtues. Once, alone, I found myself in tears. It was, I discovered, a moment many others had also experienced, as if we were holding a private wake for a university, or the idea of a university, that we had cherished. The black leader who had given Cornell until nine to live on that grim Tuesday provided another explanation in a later speech. The Black Liberation Front, he said, had too much of a psychological investment in its rhetoric to change it when it came up against reality. "So the first step we took in changing reality," he explained, was to make the faculty "go through the same kind of agony and fear that we have to go through. . . . What we did was make the faculty the isolated minority."[10] No clearer statement could be made of the expressive nature of a politics that finds academic surrogates for the nightmare of "the white Devil" and the dream of a Black Nation. Under these circumstances the university becomes a stage on which to enact a revenge play to settle an ancient and terrible score.

So long as a quarter of the students and faculty polled in May think that "disruptive, even violent, take-overs" are *not* "an unjustifiable method for the expression of student griev-

[10] Willard Straight Hall, June 29, 1969. He also slanderously accused the ex-chairman of government of having vetoed the appointment of an allegedly anti-Semitic militant out of ethnic resentment as a Jew. He was not, in fact, on either of the committees that vetoed the candidate.

ances today," the crisis is not yet fully over, even under the leadership of a new President, the widely respected former Provost. Perhaps the difficulty goes deeper, into the temper of our academic life, which, for the sake of good causes, has lost the taste for argument, for dialectic, for changing one's outlook in the light of reason and evidence. The mind that can choose sides according to its truths, rather than choose its truths according to the side it has picked, is in for bad times in the winter of our discontent. Students in recent years have come to respond regularly to some lecturers, not with doubts and queries but with enthusiastic applause. But even if the applause is deserved and the truths are ones we share, we must worry when they cease to be challenged.

But we stand. Not at Armageddon and not for the Lord; divided we stand. If we can find wisdom for our condition in any fable it is that of the Libyan eagle, stricken with a dart, who said when he saw the fashion of the shaft: "With our own feathers, not by others' hands, are we now smitten."

POSTSCRIPT:
> "But what good came of it at last?"
> Quoth little Peterkin.
> "Why, that I cannot tell," said he;
> "But 'twas a famous victory."

ROBERT SOUTHEY

When the above narrative was written, it seemed necessary primarily to speak from the perspective of one's own experience *in media res*. Since then the course of events has provided a larger perspective and an ironic one. The response of the administration and faculty, under the pressure of crisis, was to sanction a general "restructuring" of the "governance" of the university. Yet the elected black delegates to the Constituent Assembly never attended any of the regular fall meetings. The appetite of white students for participating in the Assembly was notably dull, only about half of the delegates attending the sessions. On the day that the faculty voted (307–54) for the newly devised Senate, equally dividing legislative power over non-academic matters between students and faculty, an editorial in the campus newspaper fretfully hoped that rebels across the hill at Ithaca College, where a building was "occupied," would reap something more "significant and rewarding" than a Senate which appears to be the only "spoils of our turmoil."

Black students have an Africana Center with a small black faculty, ten courses for selected black students, and one course that it was persuaded to offer to all students wishing to take it. A possible confrontation, stemming from vague charges of "insensitivity" leveled by some black students at a courageously independent black assistant dean, was averted when the BLF finally chose not to agitate the issue. The palpable tension and fear of 1969 have receded.

Innovation in the curriculum has been slanted toward the present-mindedness of the young—Cuban Marxism, local social work, scientific ecology. The modern humanist who still wishes to speak for the past must be an upstream swimmer. Nor is his fate made any easier by the backlash that New Left attacks on professionalism have produced.

There are signs of decay in the radical youth movement—the collapse of SDS into factionalism and the profitable exploitation of youth culture by all the mass media. But the style of this movement, as Cornell's story demonstrates, is revivalistic—stimulated by guilt and the hunger for community, vulnerable to conspiratorial views of the "Establishment," capable of short-term displays of mass fervor and of crusading zeal with an anti-intellectual animus. At times of social dislocation and upheaval revivals have recurred in American history very much more often than rationalists ever expected. A revival aims to convert the world and defeat the forces of evil. Therefore it can have moments of triumph but it does not know how to recognize limited victories. For this reason any lull is ambiguous.

Meanwhile the mood on campus is sluggish.[11] The university is moving slowly toward putting ROTC on an extra-curricula basis for military-sponsored courses, though a divided faculty committee was unable to give any articulate rationale for its conclusions. Last year's dialogue of the deaf has given way to the sporadic speech of the "practicals" who have reaped what the radicals sowed. This move from militant rhetoric to committee prose certainly makes for relative stability, but it also suggests Tocqueville's observation about the American: "His ideas are all either extremely minute and clear, or extremely general and vague: what lies between is a void." It is that void we now need to fill—on the campus and in the country.

[11] Since then the re-escalation of the war and the brutal shooting of four students at Kent State have transformed most campuses. But it is still moot whether the current student concern for non-symbolic politics will endure. So long as the government recklessly fosters polarization here and abroad, however, it will be very hard for universities to claim the intellectual energies of the young and for professors to sustain belief in the value of their own work. In a crisis, moderate students and professors will always find it easier, unfortunately, to follow along in the wake of the wave set in motion by the radical vanguards, rather than to organize and maintain their own perspective.

THE NON-MILITANT STUDENTS

ELDON KENWORTHY

Eldon Kenworthy was born in 1935. He received his B.A. in history
from Oberlin College and has his doctorate in political science from
Yale. He has been teaching at Cornell since 1966, specializing in Latin
American politics.

> While destructiveness is limited to a very small
> number; and while romantic visions of the university
> as a misty community without form or authority are
> confined to a limited minority; impatience is
> pervasive. Right, left, bright, dull, active,
> apathetic—the shadow of impatience touches them all.
> KINGMAN BREWSTER

At Cornell the SDS and the black students' organization
(now known as the BLF) have a hundred active members
each, the SDS maybe two.[1] What gave the Cornell crisis its
particular form was the participation of several thousand
white students. At one point three thousand of them seemed
prepared to "move" on the university (i.e., occupy buildings).

[1] In the wake of the April crisis the SDS at Cornell, as elsewhere, broke into factions. "SDS is dead. Long live the Revolution!"
was seen scrawled on a wall that summer. The BLF also has been in
flux, product of a growing number of black students at Cornell and
of the creation in the fall of 1969 of a black studies center. These
estimates of active membership, rough as they are, thus, pertain
only to the spring of 1969.

Three days later another two thousand or so applauded a panel of professors who claimed that even the threat of such an action undercut academic freedom to the point where the university's existence was in jeopardy.

Confusing many people's categories, considerable overlap existed between these two groups. One of the graffiti to appear in those days read, "Silent Center, shut up!" but as the overlapping audiences suggest, what the center was saying was not altogether clear. Indeed, to some faculty, the Barton Hall community—which this group dominated—represented "fascism," while to the SDS it was the "student government types" coming out of the woodwork. What follows is an attempt to describe the events of April from the perspective of this large, modal group of involved but non-militant students. This runs the risk, naturally, of homogenizing a diverse reality.

Not just among radical activists, but among the student generation as a whole, there has been a growing disaffection with the way the university makes decisions. Product in part of this generation's faith that nothing done cannot be reversed, the students' style of resolving issues has become increasingly spontaneous and instinctual. For them, procedure has been discredited by the runaround; precise language by cant; and representation by the way many important issues have been reserved for other arenas. Over the two years preceding the crisis, student government was ridiculed out of existence at Cornell. The situation in April, then, was one in which students both demanded meaningful representation and denied that any small group of students could represent others.

What the April crisis produced was probably the only procedure that could balance these conflicting attitudes: the plebiscite. At first students stumbled onto it, when several thousand of them said to a faculty of a thousand plus, "Reverse your decision on the black students' reprimands." Because the threat of major disruption was implicit in this demand, the faculty reversed itself. Then this Barton Hall assembly of (mostly) students moved on to other issues, first timidly declaring no classes for the following few days, then exuberantly stating it would "restructure" the university. In the days that followed various resolutions were drafted and passed by the assembled Barton Hall community—and "community" was a key symbol—which fluctuated in number around the three thousand mark. (Cornell has approximately fourteen thousand students.) Those on the dais did a masterful job, for the most part, of clothing a plebiscite with a few basic parliamentary procedures.

On several issues consensus was clear. But as SDS pushed for more radical positions (half the entering freshmen to come from working-class homes) and as blacks wrung white liberal guilt dry, decision by plebiscite no longer worked. The number of proposals sent to committees increased, and the restructurers argued the priority of drafting a new university government. Change the university power structure first, they said, and then we will win on the issues. Outnumbered, the programmatic militants (black and white) left Barton Hall to the restructurers, who turned to the question of how to select delegates to a constitutional convention. Just before its numbers dwindled to the point where its legitimacy would have been undercut, the Barton Hall community established the machinery that would keep restructuring alive at least through the summer.

The faculty and administration prefer a different style of decision-making. In the past the internal governance of the university rarely has been the primary concern of either the professor or the President. Together, administrators and faculty have dispatched important issues to slow-moving committees of notables: the faculty, both to maximize deliberation and to keep public issues from taking up too much private time; the administration, to build consensus among the scattered fiefdoms that comprise Cornell. ("I would found an institution where any person can find instruction in any study," said the founder, and he did, Cornell now having fourteen separate colleges.) For example, the status of ROTC on campus had been an issue for two years, and had been passed from one blue-ribbon committee to another, before the university faculty finally voted on the key question of whether or not to keep ROTC on campus.

To understand the April crisis, then, one must glimpse not only the distance between the psychological worlds inhabited by blacks and whites, but an analogous gulf between students and professors. Most students always have assumed that they weren't as informed, rational or cultivated as their teachers. Now, however, large numbers are not sure they want to be. During the crisis I was struck by the different political experience of the two groups. Students had not experienced the Joe McCarthy era; faculty, for the most part, have not been subject to the Vietnam draft. Near the peak of the crisis, Cornell's President called a special convocation. An unprecedented number of students, perhaps ten thousand, turned out. Hearing Mr. Perkins' vacuous generalizations over the student radio station, where they interrupted such fare as the Beatles' "Why Don't We Do It in the Road?" was when I sensed that the generation gap was something more than a cliché.[2]

Some corroboration for these impressions appeared the following fall, with the publication of an opinion poll commissioned by the trustees. This poll, conducted by Douglas Williams Associates in the summer, underscored the *general* nature of the discontent that had surfaced in the April crisis:

[2] Rumor has it that President Perkins was warned, in advance of this speech, not to touch upon the actual events of the preceding weekend, because if he did so, militant students would seize the microphone in order to give their version of the same events. It is hard to know which interpretation discredits the President less: that he would permit a small group of militants to shape this crucial statement to the university at large, or that, free from such threats, he actually thought it possible to unify the community through liberal platitudes.

general in the sense of being widespread among students, and general in the sense of touching upon issues other than the manifest ones generated by black students in a white university. Over a third of the students and nearly half of the faculty described student unrest in the spring as a "ground swell," while another quarter of each group estimated that it was "somewhere in between a small minority and a ground swell." As for the issues motivating white students, the authors of the poll approvingly quote this estimation, given by a student: "I'd say about thirty per cent of the students are dissatisfied about things the leftists talk about. However, there is a widespread feeling of unrest related to faculty-student relations and to the general functioning of the university."[3]

In the wake of the crisis, not only did the non-militant "center" turn to the task of restructuring university governance, but many of them also turned to their own departments, asking for opportunities to "rap" with teachers on a number of problems. For a brief moment some departments at Cornell took on the aspect of medieval colleges, or at least of our Paul Goodmanesque, over-romanticized notion of medieval colleges. A few even formed "communes." Professors, graduate students, research assistants and undergraduates abandoned the business of the university to discuss why that business was frustrating to so many involved. Proposals for radical curricular reforms were aired, and a democratic air prevailed, which some faculty welcomed and some resented.

As Cornell approaches the first anniversary of the April crisis, it seems clear that some restructuring of university governance will be achieved, albeit in a moderate form. Still unresolved, as this is written, is the question of whether students will have an effective voice on issues other than those which the faculty, administration and trustees define as theirs: the "campus life" questions of housing, dining, parietal rules and the like. (Old-style student government floundered on

[3] "Williams Reports on Cornell Attitudes," *Cornell Chronicle*, October 23, 1969.

the inconsequence of these issues for students, once they had gained a measure of control over them, in contrast to questions of educational policy and university involvement in society.) The newly baptized University Senate promises somewhat more; how much more, however, remains unclear due to the ambiguities required for faculty, administration and trustee approval.

With the exception of the Vietnam "mobilizations," the semester following the April events found the campus quiescent and cold. Students I know who seem representative of the group described in this essay—that is, who were politically active in the crisis without being doctrinaire (left or right)—greet the new University Senate with little enthusiasm. In contrast to the perception many faculty members voiced during and after the upheaval, apparently what motivated these students to play an active role in April and May of 1969 was a desire less for power than for community. These students now know, however, that community with black students is premature; that the brief flickering of community with faculty and graduate students on the departmental level cannot withstand the return to business as usual; and that no general assembly, even though heir to Barton Hall, can prolong the community among themselves which the crisis induced.

On Monday, April 21, following President Perkins' convocation, the university faculty passed resolutions which struck many students as more self-righteous, if less platitudinous, than the President's address. For some professors, the key issue was the defense of the judicial system in which six black students had become entangled for minor offenses their organization later declared to be political in nature; for others, it was the impropriety of a faculty bowing before student pressure. What troubled many faculty members was not simply these manifest issues, of course, but their relationship to a pattern of events, past and projected, which they saw endangering academic freedom. An important aspect of the crisis, then, was the different perception by white students and faculty of the judicial system, of the black students' relation to it, of the legitimate channels open to students to express disagreement with faculty positions, and of the long-term implications of various solutions.

The judicial system had merit. As revised the year before, it probably offered students as much freedom as is possible given the fact that complete indifference to their conduct by university authorities could result only in increased supervision by civil authorities. It was, however, a code passed down from on high. Some students participated in the drafting, and five students sat with four faculty on the court it created (the Conduct Board), but the vast majority of students neither knew what the new code contained nor attributed much legitimacy to it. It was regarded as apathetically as "student government" had come to be: as just another attempt by the administration and faculty to implicate students in the task of keeping the place quiet.[4]

Thousands of white students identified with the blacks judged by the Conduct Board, not, I sensed, because they had sorted out the philosophical issues raised by black leaders: whether political acts committed by organizations should be tried as code violations committed by individuals, whether "the university" was acting as judge in a dispute to which it was a party, whether black students were indeed a part of the community that supposedly had given its assent to this system. What most white students perceived was much simpler,

[4] The Williams poll found only 15% of the student body to be "well informed" about the judicial system. This poll was taken *after* the crisis in which the judicial system was an issue. Yet over half of the students polled (55%) stated that the judicial system was "in need of serious revision." The Williams poll found both the faculty and the administration to be better informed than the students, although not spectacularly so. (Only 27% of the faculty and 32% of the administrators were characterized as "well informed.") No more than a third of these groups, however, agreed that the institution was in need of complete overhauling.

indeed too simple: that the blacks had been given the run-around in ways familiar to them from past contacts with university governance. The blacks had been given the run-around when, after several weeks of being threatened with suspension for not appearing before the tribunal, the defendants discovered written on the backs of their summonses a provision for trying cases without such an appearance. They had been given the runaround, in most white students' eyes, when the faculty refused to ratify the major concession the administration made to the blacks occupying the student union, namely that the reprimands finally given three of them by the judicial board be dropped.

Black students, to be sure, did not interpret all this merely as a runaround. They called it deliberate maliciousness, an attempt by the university "power structure" to humiliate them. Not being black, young, or recently thrust into a large white university, I don't know if this is how black student leaders really read the situation or if this was political rhetoric. (Having dealt with bureaucrats in foreign countries, I know myself to be susceptible to conspiratorial interpretations of what are in all probability absent-mindedness and honest mistakes.) For most white students it was enough that the black students had in fact been subject to the runaround and that they were in fact sufficiently angry about it to say they couldn't let the reprimands stand and peacefully remain at Cornell. Forced between making Cornell tolerable for black students and upholding three reprimands, the majority of participating white students found little difficulty in choosing the former. They could not understand why the faculty saw this choice as a moral dilemma of the first order.

The faculty would not void the reprimands in its Monday meeting because to do so, it said, would mean legitimizing force as a means of getting one's way at the university. The administration had agreed to recommend that the reprimands be rescinded, said a majority of the faculty, only under the duress presented by armed black students occupying the student union. On Wednesday, however, the faculty found itself in a similar situation. This time, however, the duress came from the presence in Barton Hall of several thousand white students who had been prepared to "move" on the university the previous night until persuaded to give the faculty another chance. As the faculty deliberated on Wednesday afternoon, five to seven thousand students awaited its decision in Barton Hall, the cavernous gymnasium where half of them had spent the previous night.

Giving the faculty another chance had not been a part of the original SDS and BLF (then AAS) scenarios. President Perkins on Monday had declared Cornell to be in a "situation of emergency": students occupying buildings would be expelled, non-students arrested, and outside police—meaning not just Ithaca's but sheriffs or state troopers—would be called in. In these circumstances the SDS held two mass rallies to insure that it would have large numbers of students with it when it moved, while the AAS apparently hesitated to expose its members without SDS backing.

Early in the Tuesday night meeting in Barton Hall some two thirds of the six or seven thousand there raised affirmative fists in response to a black leader, asking who would be with them when they moved that night. It is partially by accident— an accident in which SDS's democracy played a role—that the militants lost control of the mass meeting and the outward spiral of adhesion was reversed. That afternoon the Faculty Council had called a special meeting of the university faculty, to be held Wednesday noon, and the Council along with two college faculties had issued statements supporting a reversal of the university faculty's Monday decision. While SDS spokesmen urged those in Barton Hall who were "serious" to move to Bailey Hall where tactics for that night's action would be set, a young professor[5] grabbed the microphone to point out that these afternoon actions by faculty groups meant that "moving on the university" was no longer the only alternative open to those who identified with the

[5] The author of this essay.—Eds.

black students' demand that the reprimands be voided. "Rational radicals," he said, could afford to await the outcome of the next day's faculty meeting. Around this time the mood of the Barton Hall audience shifted, and calls of "don't go" followed the small faction of SDS students who left the dais headed for Bailey Hall. Very few of the audience left, despite the raised fists earlier.

Seeing that most of the gathering was no longer with SDS in its plans to "move" that night, one of its leaders adroitly redefined the plans to suit majority sentiment. The Barton Hall meeting could be the occupation, he pointed out, if those there remained through the night, until either President Perkins came down to explain his stand or the faculty acted the next day. Shortly afterwards, the black student leaders postponed their deadline. (Earlier, one had given the university "until nine to live.") All this occurred on the night of April 22, Lenin's birthday. The Mensheviks had won, and Cornell averted what well might have been serious bloodshed. A black spokesman had implied his group would be armed "for self-defense"; a few fraternities were known to keep several guns "for hunting"; and the restraint of the local sheriffs or state troopers whom the administration intended to call in was, to put it generously, an unknown factor.

Whether Barton Hall was "occupied" that night or not is a matter of definition. The pressure the faculty felt as it voted the next day hardly would have been less had that number of students awaited the outcome in the open air of the Arts quadrangle. No important university business was stopped, no one was prevented from entering or leaving Barton Hall. The spirit of those who stayed is exemplified by the efforts many students made the next morning to find their teachers and *explain* to them why the reprimands should be dropped.

In reversing itself the next day, most faculty members only admitted that, if forced to choose between their principles

and avoiding what one professor[6] later called a descent into
a Hobbesian state of nature, they would opt for the latter.
After the vote nullifying the reprimands, several resolutions
were introduced; one refreshingly couched in ordinary language which said to the student body, "We hear you." It
passed, I'm not sure why, for it seemed to imply—as the
mood of the meeting did not—that the faculty saw something
besides high principle and brute force in the situation, i.e.,
some of the underlying problems of black-white and student-
faculty alienation.

The dominant mood of the faculty, on the other hand,
seemed to say, "We have bought time to explain to you mis-
guided students why your massing in Barton Hall was a
threat to the very being of the university." An even more
aggressive tone was set by some professors who interpreted
the demonstration of student power as fascism, drawing
analogies both to Germany in the thirties and to America in
the McCarthy era. By interposing themselves between the
militants and the faculty, the bulk of the Barton Hall students
felt they had staved off violence and thus acted responsibly.
They were dismayed by the capsulated news stories which
projected an image of Barton Hall as a carnival of power-
crazed youths. The newspaper and the television set were the
nearest most faculty members came to Barton Hall, of course,
which may account for the quips about the Barton and
Bailey Circus and the irresponsible talk about fascism.

The large mass of white students had let the university
down, the professors said, in not realizing that, if guns and
threats to occupy buildings are used to force the faculty to
reverse itself on matters affecting the judicial system, they
might be used to similar ends on matters affecting academic
freedom. There is certainly truth to the claim that tactics
successful in one arena *may* be transferred to another, or

[6] Milton Konvitz, "Why One Professor Changed His Vote," *New
York Times Magazine*, May 18, 1969.

that *once* the hiring and firing of teachers or the choice of course content are decided by plebiscite, the university is finished. But weren't the students trapped in guilt-by-anticipation? How did the faculty *know* they couldn't distinguish academic freedom issues from others? Was this, in fact, not a sophisticated put-down, a way of preserving faculty prerogatives on a whole range of issues in which academic freedom is not implicated or, if implicated, implicated in ways capable of more than the faculty's interpretation?

Several professors, especially in the politically sensitive disciplines of government and history, claimed that damage to academic freedom was no mere future possibility but present fact: already they felt compelled to edit lectures or to avoid teaching certain subjects. Again, several students with whom I talked expressed bewilderment, even anger, at this position. Was it not a self-fulfilling prophecy? If one doesn't teach what he otherwise would because of anticipated disruptions, a loss of academic freedom becomes a certainty even though the real attack on it was only a probability. In at least one instance, a group of students tried to induce a resigning professor to reconsider by promising that they personally would protect his right to say whatever he wanted to in the classroom. This, however, failed to change his mind.

The academic freedom issue was muddied, I believe, by the faculty's inability to separate the essential conditions of academic freedom from the more nebulous conditions for good teaching from the still broader conditions for faculty comfort. What we on the faculty failed to do, I believe, was make clear our preference for not having to act heroically, as well as to convince students that, given this preference, most of us are not effective teachers under heroic conditions. These personal and pedagogical needs, however, were swathed in the glowing rhetoric of academic freedom. "Self-censorship" provided the link between the two. Consider, for example, this statement by Allan Sindler in a paper delivered to the American Political Science Association the fall following the crisis. (Professor Sindler resigned from the Cornell faculty after the Wednesday vote reversing the faculty's Monday position.)

> When the environment for academic freedom is insufficiently supportive, as it recently has become at Cornell, the typical accommodation of a faculty man will be to play it safe, to teach students what they want to hear and will accept. Such faculty self-censorship undercuts academic freedom more pervasively and effectively than do the more dramatic incidents of disrupting classrooms, interrupting speakers, and the like.

Few are heroic in any profession—but fewer still will proclaim the fact.

Without being quite so cynical, one might note that many professors use the classroom to refine their thinking, to explore a new train of thought—to say, in a word, things they are not yet willing or able to defend. If the term is strictly defined, academic freedom probably does not protect this activity. (I interpret the teacher's academic freedom in the classroom as his freedom to say anything germane to the course that he *is* willing to defend.) It certainly does not exempt a professor from being challenged by students who take seriously the implications his remarks, offhand though they may be, hold for social issues or for personal identity. In an atmosphere of student challenge, what many professors edit out of their courses are precisely these trial runs. On the one hand, one can welcome this development as more responsible teaching. (If we wouldn't publish it, should we be saying it from the lectern?) But on the other hand, it is hard not to feel that something of value is lost for the student as well as the professor when teaching no longer has an element of spontaneity and intellectual play. (If one has already published it, why say it?) This dilemma might be averted if professors made no pretense of being authoritative, but in those circumstances it would be hard for them to deny students with conflicting views "equal time" inside the classroom, something few professors are willing to do.

Instead, however, of talking realistically about how they function, most faculty members either called up memories of the embattled leftist teachers of the McCarthy era or spun out images of some Newmanesque university that Cornell never was, at least not in the years I have known it. Forced to define the conditions for academic freedom, faculty members fell back on elaborate abstractions which translated out as "whatever makes a faculty man comfortable." Repeatedly, the McPhelin incident of the previous spring was resurrected to chart the beginning of the fateful trend leading to the April events—and repeatedly, faculty failed to consider that in that unhappy situation the academic freedom of McPhelin's *students* had been as much at issue as that of the professor. Not unsurprisingly, the Williams poll discovered that 62% of the Cornell faculty defined academic freedom in terms applicable to the faculty alone, while only a fourth included a more than token student component in their definition.

Confronted with the faculty's inability either to talk convincingly about the real, psychological conditions for effective teaching or to include in the abstract discussion of academic freedom recognition of student rights, many students came to view the whole issue as a red herring, as merely a part of the ideological superstructure faculty use to dismiss effective student pressure on any important issue. Representative of this view is a column in the student newspaper, taking up this aspect of the April crisis from the perspective of ten months' elapsed time.

> Couched in classic liberal polemic, arguments reaffirming the inviolability of academic freedom were attempts to defend and legitimize the power and position of the medieval oligarchs of the university—the faculty. Academic freedom . . . represented an attempt to defend the con-

cept of privilege, of class, and to perpetuate a basically
autocratic view of the world still endemic to much American thinking.[7]

Hard and simplistic language, but not an unexpected response
to the way many faculty members, caught up in the crisis,
subsumed all issues under the single question—Our academic
freedom, yes or no.

For other students of the large group I have loosely cate-
gorized as the active center, the resignations of respected
teachers and the refusal of many more to teach the remainder
of the semester elicited a more complex response. Had they,
the students, been shortsighted, insensitive to real but dimly
perceived preconditions for the kind of teaching they admired?
While uncomfortable with the analogy, many students clearly
were troubled when Professor George Kahin, whose early
stand opposing the Vietnam war they admire, accused them
of letting "racist" be used the way "Communist sympathizer"
had been in the fifties. But before these students could sort
matters out, summer vacation intervened and fall brought
business as usual, including the usual absence of discussion
about academic freedom. The Williams poll found student
perceptions of academic freedom scattered among several alternatives, 33% defining it largely in faculty terms, another
30% as a "two-way street" involving both faculty and students, while 17% saw it primarily in terms of student rights.

[7] Mark Goldman, "On Academic Freedom," *Cornell Daily Sun*,
February 20, 1970.

APRIL 1969: A CELEBRATION OF THE MASS

HOWARD M. FEINSTEIN

Howard Feinstein was born in 1929. As an undergraduate at Cornell, he majored in history. After graduating, he entered the Cornell Medical School, and then completed training in psychiatry. He now combines private practice with graduate work in the Department of History at Cornell.

Our turn had come; feared, anticipated, but uninvited, the paroxysm of student rebellion ruptured the façade of springtime tranquillity at Cornell. The inevitable swarm of newsmen and photographers came to watch us flail and stagger on the edge of the abyss and then make copy to astound and horrify the rest of the country. They filmed frantic meetings and reported the accusations and manifestos that chronicled revolt. But they did not tell our pain. "I went off by myself and cried," a friend confided. "It was one of the saddest days of my life," said another. We struggled with it in our waking and our lying down. "I couldn't get to sleep—it was just there all of the time. I dreamed about it. It was the first thing on my mind when I opened my eyes in the morning," a bearded student told me. Some smoked pot and drank to turn it off; others feared letting go for a moment. The world seemed to be caving in around us. Even the buildings lacked substance. "I expected to be able to put my hand through the stone," was the comment of a young faculty member. There was no longer any place to hide. Berkeley, Columbia, Harvard —they knew. Now we did too.

How does one explain the development of a revolutionary crowd of eight to ten thousand that toppled all symbols of faculty and administrative authority and turned an ordinarily orderly college campus to anarchy? How could one understand the magnitude of our pain—or our exhilaration? I attempt this analysis from the dual vantage point of a psychiatrist and a graduate student in history at Cornell. It is based on interviews in a clinical setting and a tape-recorded seminar of three two-hour sessions which I arranged for history graduate students interested in the emotional impact of the crisis and a taped session with a group of "the Concerned Faculty." My conclusions will startle no one. Hobbes, Locke, Freud, Le Bon, to cite a few, have told it all before, but this was a moment in our lives and revived the jaded texts.

Primary of course is the fact that the occupying students were black. The university administration, under the leadership of President Perkins, had committed itself to help alleviate the plight of young blacks in this country by recruiting black students for Cornell. The faculty and student body generally supported this effort. Liberals and radicals united to help "right the wrongs of three hundred years of slavery." In this mood there was an inclination to treat the most vocal blacks (or the most threatening) as spokesmen for the entire black student group who would define the next steps necessary for their "liberation." In effect this set up an alliance between the most militant blacks and the white liberals. Administrative concessions to black militant demands were eventually viewed as attacks on "racism." The merit of specific issues tended to get lost and after a time were lumped into the general category of "legitimate black needs." "Meet the Black Demands! Fight Racism! Meet the Black Demands! Fight Racism!" was the chant of the crowd.

Equally important was the fact that they were students. The occupation was tied to the issue of student power. As the most visible representatives of the "Establishment," the university faculty is looked upon as conservative when faced with student demands for university reform. With the administration negotiating secretly with a student group to define the structure of a proposed black college, an alliance was established between administration and students against the faculty. In spite of the fact that the judiciary system was drawn up as a joint student-faculty venture and the Board was comprised of students and faculty, the imposing of any penalties at all was seen as an attack on students' rights to "control their own destiny." As the events of the occupation advanced, the faculty was put into a progressively more untenable position by the administration and the radical-led students. Men whose expertise is reading, writing, and talking about books found themselves looking at the barrels of student-held guns.

If one had to point to a single element in the network of forces that produced the revolutionary situation at Cornell, I would point to the introduction of arms into the black-occupied building. This was critical, not because the guns were in the hands of blacks (as the AAS charged) but because it was powerfully symbolic of the complete erosion of authority in the university. When the blacks occupied the Straight, the administration was slow to respond. The few campus patrolmen on duty at the building kept watch on what went on and nothing more. Shortly after 9:00 A.M. a small group of athletes from a nearby fraternity house broke into the Straight. They apparently entered at a point where black women were among the first people they met. The screams of fear and surprise brought defending black men to the scene, and the whites were thrown out of the building. The theme of white attacks on black women had been introduced by a cross-burning in front of the black women's cooperative the night before the occupation. It was reinforced here again and was later very important in the rhetoric of the blacks as they explained their violent stand.

It is a powerful symbol of a past sense of impotence. It has emotional power too because black women are a source of conflict for those men trying to make the shift from integration to black power. As a part of the previously more highly valued culture, the white woman was more desirable. Yet to forsake black women for white women was a slur on a man's own blackness. "Defending our women" became doubly important because it emphasized a new-found sense of strength and a new willingness to value blackness.

The administration's failure to assert control of the situation soon after the occupation left open the possibility that a counterattack by white students would occur. When this took place there was still no effort to master the situation. One of the black leaders called to an administrator standing outside the Straight, "Mr. ———, You've got to protect us. You've got to keep kids away. You've got to do something." He was told, "Look, Ed. You got yourself into this bag. We're doing the best that we can." That "best" did not include using police to control movement of blacks or whites in and out of the Straight.

Fear played an important role in creating the crowd. It was easy to be frightened, and the fear was contagious. SDS spent the night guarding the entrance to the building against "fraternity boys." One of them told me, "I hope the faculty does something fast about getting rid of the reprimands. The blacks in there are really frightened." I don't know what the blacks were feeling, but it was clear to me that the SDS guard himself was afraid. I began to feel afraid too. As I reached the front of the building, there was a small group of students and faculty milling around to show support for the blacks inside. I saw a huge crowd heading toward us and immediately thought that the feared massacre was about to begin. It wasn't until they came close enough for me to hear their chants and see the fists being waved in the air in the sign of black power that I knew my mistake. It was a sympathetic crowd and not the feared "fraternity boys."

The "fraternity boys" who were imagined to be organizing a mass assault were terrified themselves. Some houses mounted armed guards in the trees to ward off anticipated attacks from avenging blacks.

In this atmosphere of contagious fear, the administration opened negotiations with the blacks. They aimed to get the blacks to leave the Straight as soon as possible to avoid an accidental gun battle. Throughout Saturday night reports kept coming in of groups of "fraternity boys" drinking at the local bars and preparing for an assault. A call from SDS to the blacks in the Straight warned them of an impending attack. But there was none. The administration entered into the fear of imagined attackers. As far as I have been able to determine, the only attacks on the blacks were made by a handful of unarmed students before the guns were brought in. Though guns were undoubtedly in the hands of many whites in the county, there is no evidence that a racial massacre was brewing.

This is an important point to emphasize because it shows how the paranoid style adopted by militant blacks functions as a self-fulfilling prophecy. By using the word "paranoid" I do not mean that the blacks are ill. Rather, I use it to point to a constellation of suspiciousness, heated exaggeration, and conspiratorial fantasy combined with righteousness and moral indignation that has a long history in American politics. (I follow Richard Hofstadter in this usage.) The militant blacks say that institutionalized racism threatens the destruction of black people. All whites are presumed to hate blacks and desire their destruction. In this view, militant acts of threatened and actual violence are justified as attempts to change the status quo and to avoid genocide. When militant acts such as the Straight occupation occur, they provoke acts of counteraggression like the attempted invasion by a handful of white students. These are taken by the blacks as proof of white racism and justify further militant actions such as the acquisition of guns "for defense." The introduction of

guns makes the whites reach for their guns and this is seen
as further proof of the genocidal conspiracy. That the blacks
have been oppressed is beyond question, as is the fact that
many people are intensely prejudiced against them. But it is
extremely doubtful that the hills of Tompkins County
abounded with vigilantes who were ready and anxious to
destroy Cornell's black students.

But the administration accepted this "paranoid" point of
view and negotiated within the climate of that acceptance.
Vice President Steven Muller, who was one of the negotiators,
later denied it took place at gun point or that he had been
intimidated into agreeing to support nullification of the reprimands by the faculty. It is true that no weapon was pointed
at him as he talked, but the presence of guns and the paranoid
context into which they were introduced forced him to act
as a suppliant trying to avoid bloodshed. This put him at
the mercy of the black students' fears and the black students'
guns. Thus he agreed to let them come out with their guns
because "they were threatened and wanted the weapons."
The picture of blacks emerging from the Straight carrying
guns and wearing bandoliers was one more public demonstration that the Perkins administration lacked authority. Guns
ruled Cornell. Once again Perkins' liberal administration with
the most humane intentions—the sparing of human life—
acted in such a way as to form a functional alliance with
black militants, and once again it put the faculty out on a
limb.

At 9:00 A.M. the following morning President Perkins
made his first public appearance since the occupation by
personally announcing over the radio that guns would not be
allowed to be carried on campus and that the occupation of
buildings for coercive purposes henceforth "must cease." Students violating these rules would be automatically suspended.
He announced that extra police were available to enforce his
ruling. This was the first time that the President had *publicly*
assumed charge of the situation. I emphasize this fact be-

cause it is my impression that the administration failed to understand the symbolic function of its leadership. The functioning of a bureaucracy as large as the Cornell administration requires complex decision making and cannot be the province of any single individual. Anyone aware of the diffusion of power between faculty, administration, and trustees recognizes that nobody "controls" an event like the Straight occupation. But there is an important sense in which political leaders derive power in excess of their legal powers by virtue of the symbolic functions they serve. We endow leaders, particularly in times of crisis, with the power to create the impression that we are still part of a meaningful group and not a collection of individuals who have to fend for themselves.

By submitting himself to public and private humiliation as the symbolic leader of the entire community President Perkins invited the militants to treat the entire community that way. For six months he had unwittingly contributed to the erosion of one of the profound fictions that makes society possible. During the crisis he may have been working behind the scenes, but he was invisible and managed to create the impression that the university had no leader. As politicians have always known, a group wants a leader and a frightened group craves one.

The effect of his announcement on Monday morning was immediate. Even at this late stage he had the power to assume control and reduce fear. Naturally the interpretation of his action depended on one's political point of view. The radicals balked at the declaring of "martial law." Yet one radical student told me, "That's the end. Daddy's going to clamp down on us and we've no hope. We're powerless to do anything else." A more conservative graduate student commented, "When I heard that come over the radio I felt a lot better. At last he's going to do *something*." President Perkins called a university-wide convocation for that afternoon.

More than nine thousand people crowded into Barton Hall

to hear the President tell them his view of what had happened at Cornell during the past forty-eight hours and what he planned to do about it. Students, faculty members, administrators, janitors, secretaries all came to hear him. They sat in respectful silence, then bored silence, as he talked for half an hour without once mentioning the occupation. In my interviews I have not found one person who was satisfied with that performance.

> I was expecting the guy to finally get up and say something. He gets up and puts out that goddamned high school graduation speech and I was infuriated. That guy had nine thousand people ready to go. He had them right in the palm of his hand. That was a shattering experience.

A radical graduate student reported that the administration contacted all kinds of people on Sunday night about the idea of having a convocation.

> I only know the radical people that he contacted. And everybody said, "Yeah!!" From all that I can gather all sides said, "Of course! This is the time to say *something.*"

It is my impression that President Perkins' Monday convocation was the second major element in the evolution of the revolutionary crowd. The appearance of guns and the evident inability of the administration to maintain order eroded the idea that Cornell had a competent leader. The Monday convocation confirmed that impression. Furthermore it set the precedent of a university-wide crowd in the very building that was to house many of the same people the following night. But the next time they had leadership. Perkins counted himself out, and the way was left open for the AAS and the SDS to fill the gap.

As the faculty filed out of Bailey Hall on Monday afternoon, having refused to nullify the reprimands, the radicals filed in for a mass meeting. Bailey Hall was full. Skip Mead, an AAS leader, was welcomed with wild applause. Students jumped up and waved their fists in the air in the sign of black power. One professor noted apprehensively that "the crowd wanted blood." Skip Mead gave an impassioned speech, claiming that the AAS had made history marching out of the Straight with guns. "We are revolutionaries," he announced triumphantly. Two thousand students shouted approval and voted a condemnation of the faculty resolution. Speeches by Eric Evans and Tom Jones affirmed the AAS determination to "move" and urged the radical whites to move with them.

This was the first large meeting following the abdication of leadership by Perkins, and it was clear that diverse elements of the campus were forming into a radicalized mass. A series of separate issues had coalesced into a single point of confrontation. The issue of the Conduct Board's judgment had been made to seem like a fight between those who would oppress blacks and those who would aid in their liberation. The issue of student freedom to determine their "own destiny" seemed to hinge on faculty nullification. The issue of a legal community had been made to look like a choice between blind legalism and compassion for the oppressed and the faculty were made to look as if they were with all those forces that would oppress the colored minorities and the young throughout the world.

Special note must be taken of the dual usage of the threat of violence at this stage of crowd formation. Throughout the previous six months, the threat of violence was essential to radical strategy. The radicals succeeded in creating a mood of fear which brought attention to their claims and rapid administrative action. Their occupation of Willard Straight Hall with guns increased the threat of violence, yet the excitement of near violence brought out the spectators. Because the administration failed to act decisively to perform the most rudimentary act of government—peace-keeping—the radicals who earlier supported the intimidation of the campus by the AAS were able to act as the protectors of the blacks and the sole guardians of the peace. Saturday morning, instead of the police, SDS cordoned off the building to prevent a feared racist onslaught. An SDS handbill alleged that Perkins' declaration of "martial law only increases the chance of unnecessary violence, something we all wish to avoid." With Orwellian double-think the SDS-AAS alliance was able to threaten violence and claim to be the protector of the community from that very threat. Those students who had held back from the radicals' violent tactics easily embraced their peaceful aims. Radical students who embraced violence as essential to their revolutionary aim to destroy the university and moderates who abhorred the neo-fascist style of the new left and aimed to defend the university found themselves sitting side by side in an overflow SDS meeting on Tuesday night in Barton Hall.

The SDS had originally planned their meeting for a much smaller auditorium. As the crowds jammed into first Goldwyn Smith and then Bailey Hall it was evident that larger space was needed. Only the largest building on campus would accommodate them. As in any revolution, there were accidents which helped the radicals succeed. Fortunately for them, the Dean of Students had arranged for Barton Hall and other large meeting rooms on campus to be free for students from Monday on—he had anticipated large forums during the crisis. A sound system had been rented for President Perkins' speech on Monday afternoon, and it was still in Barton Hall and easily made operational on Tuesday night. By this fortuitous combination of circumstances the crowd had a warm, dry, spacious place to meet on a rainy evening and a superb amplification system to hear the radical orators vie for its leadership.

The mood of the meeting was tense. One student recalled,

"It was like just before a thunderstorm. You could just sense in that oppressive atmosphere that there was dynamite in there." Tom Jones, a leader of the AAS, knew how to take advantage of it. His speech was repeatedly referred to afterwards as the most memorable and the most terrifying oratory of the crisis. With the adroitness of the gifted mover of crowds he stated the black position. He accused the faculty of valuing their principles more than the lives of black students. He berated President Perkins and the faculty for distorting the idea of community. Community could mean only that the students who were the majority of the university community should rule the university. The faculty could not have a veto, and the President could not declare martial law. Black students were going to determine the priorities that ordered their own lives. "Cornell University," he warned, had "until nine to live."

One could learn much about the art of political rhetoric from a close analysis of his address. He threatened violence, but in a soft voice; he bobbed and weaved, riding the sound of words like "community" and "self-determination," "slavery" and "freedom," "principle" and "racism," which tapped the crowd's sympathy for the blacks at one moment and their fear of the blacks at the next. He spoke violently but said it was the whites who were violent. He demanded absolute freedom for blacks, a minority, yet in the next breath he called on the ethos of democracy and majority rule to justify the overthrow of the faculty and administration. In short he cemented the crowd through fear and confusion.

Tom Jones scared the Bejeezus out of me. It wasn't the rhetoric because I'd heard all of that before. It was the tone. Fear, determination, deadly seriousness all wrapped together. I just knew when he said he was ready to die he meant it. That was the only time that I was physically afraid.

The reaction to Jones's speech was similar whether the listener was in favor of his position or skeptical of it. A young faculty member who supported the black position described his reaction:

> Tom Jones left everybody in some kind of lack of equilibrium. He left me afraid, yet marveling at the rhetoric. He is a fantastic rhetorician who can slide from the most chilling sorts of things with hardly any modulation at all to the most ingratiating. That left everybody not knowing where they were or what was going on. I felt a chilling ball of fear in my guts listening to him.

Jones had the crowd, and violence seemed imminent. A graduate student and dorm counselor described a literal herding together of the young people around her as Jones spoke.

> I was with a bunch of kids that had come over with me from the house. When Tom Jones started talking about those racists who would be dealt with, the kids instinctively moved a little closer to me. And I thought, "Oh, God, I'm responsible for these kids."

Though Jones was purposely vague about the ways in which racists would be dealt with, one young faculty member had the following fantasy:

> At one point a picture flashed through my mind. A machine gun was pointed at the people in the bleachers because we were opponents. It was a grand gesture, a political action which was justified because the ends justify the means.

Though the SDS and AAS had succeeded in forming a crowd that appeared to seek their leadership and in moments of wild enthusiasm seemed bent on following their direction, the radical alliance had to pay a price for moderate support. By drawing the majority of students who were not radicalized and committed to SDS and AAS goals into the mass meeting, they invited an increase in their numbers but a decrease in their effectiveness. SDS had had plans for the seizing of a building for some months. They had been debating from the time the blacks entered the Straight on Saturday whether or not to go ahead with the plan, and Tuesday afternoon they decided. They were going to move from the mass meeting.

But the moderates in the crowd who came to Barton Hall because of the avowed SDS wish to prevent violence really did not want to follow SDS in an act that might precipitate bloodshed. There were many who would shudder with Jones as he announced his willingness to die, but they wanted neither to kill him nor to die alongside him. Though the decision was made to move, the radicals had to cope with their crowd in the style of participatory democracy. Contrary to popular generalizations about mass psychology, the crowd was discriminating in its reactions to the suggestions of leadership. Sensing the reluctance of the entire body, the SDS decided to split the meeting, leaving the moderates to talk while the radicals acted. A young government professor, Kenworthy, came to the microphone at the moment that an SDS-led group headed out the door. He exhorted them to wait— pointing out that the faculty would meet the following day and reminding the group that the faculties of many colleges had already passed resolutions in favor of nullification. He declared that he would be with them if they failed to nullify on Wednesday, but now was not the time for "rational radicals" to act. The move toward the door was reduced to a trickle of SDS stalwarts. The crowd had found a leader who would lead them where they wanted to go. He bound them with a catchword that all persuasions could embrace—"rational radical." Similar to the SDS-AAS resort to and rejection of violence, the phrase "rational radical" was an ambiguous banner behind which the vast majority could rally. The previously quoted dorm counselor marked the change.

> Then when Kenworthy made that beautiful plea, I felt this tremendous sense of relief. I felt that something had broken there. Like a boil being lanced.

A small group of the SDS did go to caucus in Bailey Hall but most remained to hear David Burak propose the meeting be declared an occupation until the reprimands were nullified. He accurately sensed the extent of the crowd's willingness to confront the Establishment. They were already there so no mass exodus was necessary, and the more relaxed atmosphere which followed Kenworthy's plea made occupation of Barton Hall a happy compromise. But that's as far as the crowd would go. The mood became lighthearted as students made plans to bed down for the night.

> We occupied Barton Hall at that point. It was raining and the kids said, "Gee, we want to stay here all night but we need to go home and get our sleeping bags and our toothbrushes and our pills. We can't go a night without our pills." I took them home and brought them back. Then it became sort of a picnic.

A feeling of cohesiveness and good-fellowship settled over the hall as the crowd broke into smaller discussion groups. They collected money to buy food, which was shared with all who remained. A professor noted, "The quieter Barton Hall became, the more you had the feeling of communality and partnership." A radical faculty member noted the unusual glow on the faces in that crowd:

> When the air was sufficiently electric and you did not know where things were going but you were simply keep-

ing your antennae up to take part in and to understand
what was going on, people looked different. It seems to
me that it is only at moments of crisis that people have
that look. I saw it at the Pentagon and at some private
events in my life. There is a glow over people. They look
like figures in a frieze or a historical painting. I now see
why Delacroix painted that way. People take on the
appearance of romance. Actual events have become historical, romantic.

Though they returned to Barton Hall after their caucus,
the more extremist members of SDS were angry at having
lost what turned out to be their final opportunity to lead a
mass of the student body toward a hoped-for confrontation
with the police. The blacks put off their deadline until the
next day.

Later that evening President Perkins sent word to Barton
Hall that he had recommended that meetings between students be facilitated: the meeting was officially approved and
could not be considered a seizure. Some students groaned,
others laughed. The head of the housing and dining department appeared about midnight with a food cart loaded
with sandwiches to sell at cost to the students spending the
night. He was puzzled at the lack of enthusiasm the students
showed for his well-intentioned offering. Though minor, these
incidents indicate a quality of administrative misunderstanding of a fundamental element in confrontation politics as
practiced by youth. In seeking a confrontation, young people
are most assuredly aiming at political change, but they are
also looking for the challenge and excitement and sense of
their growing powers that come from grappling with those
they have learned to think of as stronger than themselves.
They are trying to locate themselves by finding out where
their elders "are at." It is my impression that the administration consistently acted to frustrate any rite-of-passage experience for the students by repeatedly blurring the differences

between students and the Establishment. By saying, "This is no building seizure but an officially sanctioned meeting," by offering them food, albeit at cost, the ritual trial of a youth staked in the woods and left to brave the spirits of the night was made to seem about as dangerous as a faculty luncheon.

The following afternoon the faculty reversed itself and agreed to nullify the reprimands. Many professors changed their Monday vote. One who reflects, I think, a large segment of opinion explained his position:

> At the point when I saw two to three thousand students ready to move out of Barton Hall to seize a building I reversed my position. I decided that we should nullify as an act of prudence. It was clear that the faculty position had been completely misunderstood. The faculty thought it was drawing a clear line of principle, but there was no point standing by that line when nobody even saw it as a line.

But in the highly volatile atmosphere of social breakdown, an act may have a symbolic meaning that is quite different from the intent of the actor. What may have seemed an act of prudence to the faculty was interpreted by most as a final act of capitulation of established authority at Cornell. The last vestige of resistance had crumbled, and authority fell to a crowd that had been spawned by fear.

The emotional intensity generated by the events surrounding the occupation of Willard Straight Hall was enormous and requires an explanation. Clearly, there is a resonance between individual psychological integrity and social order. We function as part of a social network on the assumption that others around us know their roles and will act in predictable ways that articulate with our own. When the social order begins to disintegrate and authority falls to the mob, an individual's sense of wholeness may be undermined. He cannot continue to act on the assumption that others will mesh easily with him. The simplest meeting between friends becomes a new situation: What side is he on? Will he shake my hand or spit in my face? Can I trust him? One's social controls, which ordinarily are supported and reinforced by the imagined approval of established authorities, are suddenly without support. If buildings are occupied, guns brandished, presidents unseated, what will they do next? What will I do next?

In the atmosphere of impending chaos the discussion of issues is no longer a simple exchanging of words, but a matter of life or death. In this sense, we were all up against the wall. It is a position from which some are converted to a new sense of wholeness and others are broken.

A graduate student sat watching a televised newscast with his wife. The picture of blacks carrying guns out of the Straight flashed on the screen. He was irritated at the extremity to which the blacks had gone and said so to his wife. She told him "violence is part of life" and he "would just have to get used to it." He became enraged, pulled her out of her chair and threw her to the ground. Then he started to choke her.

A radical faculty member experienced a sense of exhilaration.

During the fall and the middle of the winter . . . I was tense, jumpy, and scared. I thought of the blacks as violence-prone and unpredictable, and I was holding things down both internally and externally. This was turning me fearfully conservative in ways that I didn't like. But the minute the Straight was occupied all this blew away. I felt restored to the old Pentagon identity again. I slept like a baby when I did sleep. I was full of energy and could have gone on forever. I felt euphoric and youthful . . . It was a great relief. I felt sane in a way that I hadn't for months.

A young scientist connected the beginning of a manic excitement with a faculty meeting at which a black professor publicly challenged President Perkins.

> I was sitting close to the front and I saw the President's face and neck flush. I identified with that black professor. It felt like I was putting Perkins down too.

In the period of successful revolution (from Tuesday to Saturday) a most striking phenomenon was the spontaneous appearance of a multitude of new political-action groups (the Committee of 41, the Concerned Faculty, Students for a Democratic Alternative,[1] and many others). The campus was flooded with mimeographed flyers. Individual departments formed a nucleus for some to congregate; chance encounters were the basis for others. Whatever the focus, Cornellians went looking for a place in which to cluster and a group to be with.

> All during the day, whenever I wasn't sitting with somebody, I was looking for someone to be with, to have a cup of coffee with, to share something, anything. I didn't care what.

It was as if the social breakdown of the Establishment made people feel vulnerable, made them sense their loneliness and isolation. They felt helpless as single individuals to influence what was going on around them. They wanted to huddle together for warmth, to band together for action, to organize to try to replace what had broken down, or try to keep from breaking down themselves.

> At one of the departmental meetings a colleague said that we had to cease being free-floating intellectuals and become political cadres. I thought that was a beauti-

[1] The author of this essay was an organizer of this group.—Eds.

ful description of what we had to do. It was with a sense
of relief that we organized a teach-in and called together
our graduate students. We were doing that as cadres.
We were only ten. We will organize our sixty graduate
students and send them into the field. And each of them
will organize ten and then we will be six hundred.

The fragmentation into small groups was accompanied by
a frantic search for leadership. The same dynamics that put
the AAS and the SDS in a position to control the crowd set
the multitude of small groups trying to fill the void left by the
invisible and now illegitimate administration.

A graduate assistant reported the following episode in a
history class:

> LaFeber stopped teaching class and the kids were mad.
> So they called a class. They were going to vote on
> whether or not to have a test. They decided they didn't
> want a final or grades for the term. One of the kids
> was up leading it, and they were going to have a vote.
> It was all very revolutionary. The minute LaFeber walked
> in—I was the only one who knew he was coming—loud
> applause broke out. He sat calmly on the desk and ex-
> plained his position. It didn't seem to me any more ra-
> tional than it had from the beginning, but they ate it
> up. . . . In the end he told them they were going to take
> the test, have sections, and there would be a final, and
> he expected them to read the material. He said good-by.
> They clapped, and that was the end of the revolution.

A youthful professor of government had an experience that
reminded him of Thermidor:

> Friday about five o'clock I went into a meeting that was
> mainly for undergraduates. [. . .] I just sort of stuck my
> head in the door and then saw someone that wanted to
> talk to me so I went outside. It was a meeting of about

three hundred people. About ten minutes later someone came out and said, "The meeting is falling apart and we voted unanimously that we want you to be the chairman." I walked to the door and there was thunderous applause.

Along with the readiness to accept leadership many developed an impatience with the sluggishness of ordinary democratic procedure. The organized groups streamlined for action early. The AAS depended on a committee of five ("like a dictatorship," noted a black student), and the SDS on a committee of ten. New-formed groups struggled with parliamentary procedure and many foundered in the quagmire of Roberts' *Rules*. While they used the rhetoric of democracy to sway the crowd, the blacks seemed particularly impatient with democratic process, which moved painfully slowly or not at all. Witness this student's report:

> There was an expanded Faculty Council meeting supposedly to consider recommendations to the Barton Hall assembly. There had been a row of blacks sitting there, but they walked out supposedly because they were fed up with the "Mickey Mouseing" over motions and amendments. One black student remained. He got up and made a three-minute speech which was a straight right to the jaw. He said, "Cut out all this crap. You know what we've got to have. It's time for you to deal, man! Deal!"

Together with the emergence of small groups that characterized the phase of successful revolution was an atmosphere that can only be called paranoid. With the disintegration of a predictable world, all associations became suspect, all coincidental happenings subject to elaboration as elements in a conspiracy. Many of the small groups formed to defend themselves against imagined plots. Clearly the SDS and the AAS had some plans formulated, but they did not function in the slick Machiavellian manner that some imagined. They made their plans as they went along and had to cope with internal division as did other elements of the campus. Obviously the administration played into the hands of the radicals through ineptness and failure to understand what they were dealing with, but it stretches the imagination to believe, as some were inclined to believe, that there was direct collusion between administrators and radicals to undermine the faculty and change the present alignment of power at Cornell. For many, it was less frightening to believe in hostile conspirators than it was to face the fact that no one was in control. A young faculty member reported the following experience:

> Wednesday night there was a meeting to plan the following day for Barton Hall. Burak was there and wanted the topic to be racism and not restructuring as others suggested. [. . .] I wondered what he was up to [. . . .] Friday someone told me that Tom Jones had announced that the blacks could not join the community because the community was still racist. That was disheartening news. I looked at the back pages of the *Sun* and it had all of these proposals for restructuring. All of a sudden I thought, "Now I see why Burak was talking about racism." I tied Tom Jones and the restructuring together. They've used racism to convince everybody that because you are white you must be a racist. They've tied that in with the need for radical restructuring. To eliminate racism we had to do away with ROTC and the Center for International Studies. "They've got it." I said, "What's the point of having a teach-in? What's the point of anything? These people with their Machiavellian strategy have the university. We might as well turn in our cards and go home. We've been outclassed."

Others have observed that the paranoid style in politics invites and nurtures counterconspiratorial thinking and actions.

We see that process at work in the comments of a graduate teaching assistant.

> The first thing that occurred to me is that there are conspiracies all over the place. I never doubted that. I figured that I'm smarter than they are. I can conspire as well as the next guy. At least we didn't have SDS's problem of believing in democracy [. . .]. You see the whole sense of paranoia—we knew it was there and we exploited it. We knew there was a fear of the radical history caucus, so we used that threat to get everyone to come to our meeting. We had our meeting. It was conscious. The funny part of it was that we found they had no organization. They came to join us.

In the atmosphere of suspicion and mistrust, relations between whites and blacks became more strained and distant. I have earlier referred to the self-fulfilling prophetic quality of the black separatist position. The readiness to provoke confrontation elicited counteraggression, which was seen as proof of the original assumptions about racism. This was true in yet another sense. The mixture of aloofness and scornful hostility that characterized the new style of blacks attempting the transition from integrationism to militant separatism made it difficult for whites and blacks to talk together. Throughout the spring, the style of militancy widened the distance between whites and blacks. There were exceptional moments, like the one reported by a member of the Concerned Faculty—a moment of community with a black student who covertly grabbed his shoulder and squeezed it as a gesture of recognition of his effort to support the blacks. But the following were more typical:

> I found myself in a difficult position in a discussion class. I wanted to say something about the blacks, and they said, "You can't understand blacks." I found the

whites in the class discussion were all getting meek. It
finally occurred to me one night, "We might as well fold
up and move on somewhere else if we can't talk any
more."

Another graduate student told of being put off:

I have three black girls in my residence. If I see them on
campus individually they will speak to me. But if I see
them with any other blacks they will give me a slight
eye twitch. One of them is in the infirmary now because
of nervous tension. It's a strain on me to go and visit
her, because there are always other blacks around [. . .].
I get the feeling that I am barely tolerated. It's as if
they were saying, "Why are you here taking up our
time? We can't talk in front of you. How soon are you
going to leave?" [. . .] This is the worst part of the whole
thing.

Another described a particularly painful moment as he tried
to help a black friend who was in the early stages of a
psychotic episode precipitated by the crisis:

I was with J for an hour the night that he went to Sage
infirmary while F went to get the black girls who were
going to stay with him. I don't think I will ever forget
when those four blacks came in. There were two girls and
a young Negro doctor besides F. J was lying on the bed,
and I was sitting there just listening to his monologue.
They walked in. None of them looked at me. They all
looked at J.
     F was talking with J. He introduced the blacks. And
they started their own conversation. I was sitting there
[. . .] nobody paying any attention to me. And I was
thinking, "Should I get up and leave? Should I stay
there? Should I act humble?" I mean I didn't know what
to do.

It was funny. J had called me his guard for the last
hour. All I know is I was feeling smaller and smaller—
like I didn't know what I was doing there. And I kept
saying to myself, "But I came out of good motives"
[. . .] I didn't know what they were thinking. Maybe
they thought, "Here is a white taking care of our black
and he is condescending in the way he is taking care
of him. And this is what whites have always done [. . .]."
    J is blind, and I motioned to F as if to ask, "Should
I go?" And he motioned back without a word as if to
say, "Yes!" Not even as much as a . . . I don't want to
say I expected a thanks but it was certainly not a
thanks. . . . I made up my mind I would never get into
a situation like that again.

While there was a force that drew people into groups out
of fear of the void, there was also a euphoric sense of
brotherhood and kinship that pulled them together. Following the faculty vote for reversal on Wednesday, the crowd
in Barton Hall continued to meet as the Barton Hall Community. The mass that had united to prevent violence, that
had banded together and successfully challenged the policies
and wisdom of its elders, was now together to harvest the
yield of what they had sown. Most certainly part of the
euphoria was due to the thrill of victory and momentary
aversion of near catastrophe. Like the loyal crowd that has
witnessed their team score a winning touchdown in the final
seconds of play, they shared a bond of trial and triumph.
But this was a special contest—a contest between youth and
age, between the bearers of a new vision of the world and
those who were thought to hold to hollow vestiges of the old.
If you believe, as I do, that men who have psychotic experiences are, like artists, often in touch with fundamental
truths in their society, which most of us are moved by but
are unable to articulate, the experience of a young scientist
is enlightening. He was moved to a mood of euphoria by

vicariously participating in the public humiliation of the President. Bearing witness to and sharing in the symbolic destruction of the father, his spirit loosened from its mundane moorings and soared. All wishes seemed near realities. The successful overthrow of the external representative of authority left the superego without a reliable ally, and impulse could become action, and wish reality, without its ubiquitous restrictions. Like Freud's mythical primal horde, they who banded together to do the act were bound by their action. Sharing in the blood of the lamb, they became brothers in Christ.

I do not use either the religious or the psychoanalytic metaphor casually. There were both religious and sexual elements felt by the members of the Barton Hall Community. A student stood before the community and testified he had been a racist supporter of George Wallace before coming to Barton Hall but now saw the error of his ways and urged others to help wipe out racism in the university. A faculty member said that he had not believed that whole nations could be baptized, but he felt that was what happened when the faculty changed its vote. Under the ephemeral cloak of spiritual brotherhood, barriers dropped and a new world seemed possible, if not at hand. "I am usually afraid of professors," confided a bearded graduate student, "even though my father is one. But at Barton Hall I went right up and talked to them with no trouble at all. I feel more optimistic about there being a place for me at Cornell now."

The radicals were quite rightly suspicious of the sudden breaking out of grace. The AAS and the SDS had specific political goals to accomplish, and they feared the momentum of their revolution was going to be dissipated in a mixture of reformism (under the heading of "restructuring") and self-indulgent Christian love. One psychology professor actually suggested that the assembled multitude leave Barton Hall and go over *en masse* to the black students' headquarters as a gesture of love and brotherhood. A black speaker rejected the idea as foolish, saying that they wanted action, not a "love-in." With their gift for verbalizing the ethos of the mass in the language of their generation, SDS distributed a handbill with the boldface heading, "MASTURBATION OR INTERCOURSE?" The sexual imagery accurately characterized a sensual element in the spirituality of the Barton Hall Community.

Throughout the crisis, emotional reactions to issues of group solidarity were intensified. A considerable amount of anger was directed against people who were felt to have violated the trust of friendship, the allegiance of race, or to have betrayed loyalties to colleagues as members of the academic guild. A visiting professor accused the radical members of his seminar, faculty and students alike, of being Nazis and threw them out of his class for betraying the freedom of the academy. He and many others were particularly outraged by a group called the Concerned Faculty which voted to occupy a building in support of the black students' demands. Professor David Lyons gave a wildly applauded speech at the Tuesday night meeting in Barton Hall in which he announced the pledge to seize a building. He began, "At the present moment, I am ashamed of being a faculty member at Cornell." This elicited the following reaction from a graduate student:

> I was five times more bitter toward that man than toward Tom Jones. That was the most highly irresponsible, irrational, inflammatory nonsense I had ever heard. . . . Faculty members taking over a building—this is a variety of treason to me. Faculty are the people who are supposed to be running the university and not tearing it apart.

Among the blacks there was considerable pressure to declare one's solidarity with the black community as defined by the AAS. Some of this was by physical threat, but for many it was an issue of identification with or participation in the Straight take-over. The pull between integration and separatism that tore at blacks throughout the year culminated in confrontation. A white student described this encounter with two blacks in front of the Straight:

> We walked on the line together. He is from Long Island. He said that he has never been in the ghetto. He doesn't know what it means. He really doesn't understand these blacks when they talk about the awful things "we've" been through. He would like to be with them but he can't be. He'd like to be inside but he can't. He's not even sure he can walk around in the picket line.
>
> The other black student is much darker. He was very hostile toward the blacks who were in there. He's a pre-professional student. He thinks this is absolutely the wrong way to go about things. He's had nothing to do with them all year. In fact he was with a white girl.

As the social breakdown accelerated, mildly competing allegiances magnified into painful conflict. A history student who also held a minor administration post found herself torn between allegiance to the administration and its handling of the blacks and her allegiance to her department, which was extremely critical of the administration.

> I'd been able to balance roles off last year. It's like having a bunch of mortgages or debts. You can keep paying off the different ones, but what are you going to do when they all come due at once? Zap! . . . My chairman expected 100% loyalty from me as a graduate student in this thing. The administration also expected 100% loyalty from me from the administration point of view [. . .]. The crux of the thing was whether I supported Perkins. [. . .] The low point came just before the Government Department teach-in on Friday. I had a

fight with my chairman—well, he raised his voice to me.
I sat on the slope outside the White Art Museum looking
out over the daffodils and wept and wept and wept.

For many, the pull of conflicting allegiances at a time of
increased demand for group solidarity was painful. For some,
it was a rack that stretched them taut until they broke.
One black, who was an extremely conscientious student, was
involved in research that made him dependent upon a number of white fellow students and student wives. He was also
very close to his white professors, who showed special interest in his growth as a scholar. Following the Straight take-
over, his chairman threatened resignation, as did other respected faculty who had been close to him. He was not inside
the Straight with the AAS but wished that he had shown
solidarity with his "brothers." He wanted to be militant and
strong and black. He wanted to be independent and competent and a scholar. A letter published in the *Cornell Sun*
reveals the painful sense of being split between divergent
worlds that would culminate in psychosis:

> It is seldom that a people is called upon to preserve
> their identity, while at the same time to question even
> the existence of that identity. This is especially true
> of a thinking, reasoning people. It is tragic, however,
> that we, the members of this community, must continue
> under present conditions to question and to assert—to
> think, to reason. (Alas, to be able not to think about the
> things which must be thought about, the luxury of a
> fool! [. . .])
> The paramount question in the back of our minds at
> this moment is—what is to be the relationship between
> complete, absolute, unquestioned academic freedom and
> black equality? Can there be a university in the absence
> of academic freedom? By the same token, can there be

complete equality in the absence of black manhood? [. . .]

To what extent does the ability of a black student to
raise and wrestle with these and other questions enable
him to protect both academic freedom and black equality—at 100% level—in a democratic as well as an academic society? (Not to mention a both peaceful and just
society?)—"I do not know!" [. . .]

Though black, I do not represent—though frequently
support—the Afro-American Society [Black Liberation
Front], Cornell University, any professor or any student.
By abstaining from all political considerations on campus,
I, unlike most students, yet retain a modicum of academic
freedom. (Can one completely abstain from political
considerations and yet retain complete academic freedom? What do these terms mean and who reserves the
right to define them?)

As the letter proceeds you can see the warring commitments
placed side by side but never resolved.

By the end of that difficult, tumultuous week the moderates of the campus had their way and the revolutionary thrust
was gone. When, after the resumption of classes, the SDS
tried to win back its revolution by pushing the issue of ban-
ning ROTC from the campus, it was barely able to muster
a crowd of three hundred to listen, and only a small fraction
of these were ready to take part in an act of interruption.
Like a muscle that requires repeated electrical stimulation
until it will contract, but then is refractory to any stimulus
for a period, the mounting tension of accumulated unresolved
challenges set off an orgiastic enthusiasm that left the campus
limp.

Racism was the issue that had explosive potential. We
live in a society that at its very beginning nearly foundered
on the issue of slavery, was brought to a fratricidal civil
war over the fate of blacks, and is still organized in a way

that exploits blacks as an underclass. The aspect of racism most pertinent to understanding its revolutionary potential for Cornell is white guilt. Many things have prepared the ground for this: a successful civil rights movement, the increasingly well-publicized decay of urban centers with their black ghettos, an affluent student body that knows the hollowness of the American dream and is aghast at the sacrifices of the blacks to bring it to realization. Whatever the reasons, white students and administrators alike could be and were made to feel guilty for the plight of the black man in America. This was a collective sense of guilt which could be tapped by the AAS for tremendous political leverage. The charge that black people have suffered for three hundred years or that our "brothers" and "sisters" in the ghetto "are crying out," if attached to any "demands," no matter how outrageous, made whites feel responsible for that suffering and those ghettos and moved them to comply. One characteristic of the youth movement is a disenchantment with the liberal concept of the individual who aims at his own self-interest and is individually responsible for his acts. In the swing toward "community" values, it is not surprising that the idea of collective guilt should appear to make sense. Yet many of the whites who were prepared to feel collectively guilty come from families who immigrated to this country long after the pattern of black exploitation was established.

There is another facet to the problem of racism that magnifies the feelings of guilt. Many of the whites at the university have lived in racially segregated white communities and have little firsthand knowledge of blacks. They have been raised in households where lip service was paid to the democratic ideal of racial equality, though there was little opportunity to experience it. The discovery that they as whites feel differently and act differently in the presence of blacks comes as a shock. The style of confrontation politics creates situations that are calculated to make the whites aware of their "unconscious" racism. The discovery can be overwhelming, for it shares the double nature of much self-revelation: relief at knowing, but also dismay at the discovery that previously unknown forces influence one's acts. The new insight may prepare the way for major political conversions that are analogous to the alterations worked toward in psychotherapy.

A young faculty member who experienced such a conversation described the experience:

> Up until the March meeting my position would have been a conservative one, negative to SDS and the black students who were given this *wonderful* opportunity and refused to accept it. It's a paternalistic approach . . . a racist thing. You don't realize you have it until it smacks you right in the face [. . .]. I went through a rather strenuous transformation during this small time period. Many of the senses that I had were in heightened form [. . .]. The only way to describe it is to compare it to an experience that I never had and I doubt that I ever will have—that people describe on certain drugs. Colors and sounds were extremely vivid [. . .]. There were relatively few periods when I was just plain happy. I had feelings of being very mad—particularly at the Establishment. Not so much at people but at the way things are ordered and difficult to change.
>
> I felt a tremendous need to get off by myself and think this through. What do I really believe? What am I willing to do? I felt hypertense, with a tremendous amount of adrenalin in my system. I needed very little sleep.
>
> I had a tremendous need to talk to people, those of my persuasion, my changing persuasion, or the opposite persuasion. I felt I had to get people to see things the way I now looked at them. I've seen this happen in religion—where a religious convert tends to go overboard at times.

Those whose discovery had less dramatic consequences were inclined to say in effect, "Give the blacks whatever they want. They are right. We are racists."

The style of politics of the civil rights movement and the peace movement is another factor that prepared the way for crisis at Cornell. The students have witnessed and participated in a social movement that has adapted the Gandhian technique of non-violence to the American political arena. As the tensions of a frustrating war and the slowness of change measured against the felt need mounted, the style shifted to a more violent one. Confrontation, the meeting face to face of opponents who share a bond of common humanity, has moved mountains, but not fast enough or often enough for the "now" generation. The young were ready to move to a style that humiliated and denigrated their opponents in the confidence that their cause was just. Having never felt the horror of moral absolutism linked with ruthless power that characterized the rise of Nazi Germany or the witch-hunting enthusiasm of the McCarthy era ("You mean Eugene?" they ask), they moved slowly but steadily to escalate (how easily the vocabulary of war comes to mind) the style of dehumanization. We were faced with the ever present problem of means and ends that is as old as politics and has to be struggled with in every generation. A graduate student who had been present at some of the first campus anti-war rallies recalled:

> I'm too young to remember Hitler. What all this reminded me of was just the tables turned from the teach-ins in the middle sixties. I went to the first teach-ins against the war. One in Wisconsin and the other at Rutgers where Genovese made his speech and we all agreed and there was wild applause after everything that was said. The only difference now is the faculty aren't up there haranguing us. But the people that they harangued were haranguing them back. Now the academic

community was being threatened instead of the government establishment [. . .]. At the Rutgers teach-in there was a guy who was supposed to defend the position of the administration. One of the anti-war speakers got really angry and interrupted him in the middle of his speech. He slammed his hand on the table so hard that his wristwatch flew into the air. Everybody screamed and hooted this guy down, and he never got a chance to finish. That was wonderful, you know, because this guy was wrong and we were right. Now all of a sudden in Barton Hall we weren't sure those kids were right because we weren't in control.

Social ordering regularizes the world in a way that may free the members of a society to lead productive and meaningful lives. But there is a constant tension between order and disorder that needs to be preserved—too much of one brings stagnation and boredom, too much of the other invites chaos. For some, the tremendous expansion of the universities following World War II and the ensuing creation of new well-salaried academic posts have provided sinecures of bourgeois regularity that they find without challenge or excitement. Boredom and the related wish for excitement ("to be where the action is") made some ready to welcome the revolution.

You are finally *there*. And that is the way the world ought to be all of the time. And everything else is just waiting around. History is where you want to be. Where you normally are is not yet in history—in some state of life that is boring.

We are not used to this alternative because we were taught in childhood that you may have your personal crises but public history does not exist. And it is startling to discover that this isn't so. Public history does exist and it can happen where you live. The moments of crisis are in fact the norm. They are only circumstantially exceptional. And that is one of the reasons that I felt relieved. I found that life was exposing itself. Things were interesting instead of uninteresting.

It must have been clear, even to people unfamiliar with universities, that an event that disrupted the community so dramatically would have an impact on the work done at Cornell. There were some obvious changes to be expected —some faculty had resigned in protest and others were looking elsewhere for a more congenial place to teach or to study. That was evident from reports in the newspapers. But what of the more important, more subtle changes that have long-term implications for the nature and survival of a university? There were ruptures of important relationships within departments that must complicate work in the future. These were not mere petty political squabbles that afflict life in any organization but fratricidal outbursts of mistrust and even hatred which must take their toll:

> I hadn't gone to faculty departmental meetings all year, so it came as a shock to see how things were coming apart. It was brother against brother. One professor walked out of the meeting and slammed the door behind him. Another called a colleague a prostitute. I was seeing society or the family just coming apart. Here were men who should be close to one another, but it was clear that there were going to be rifts which wouldn't heal for years. One professor said, "I'm not talking to you any more because you are morally contemptible." It was like non-recognition of China. Henceforth you are a non-person. . . . There were other people who had been the closest friends—one, for example, who would go into ————'s office first thing in the morning for the past nine years. He doesn't do it any more.

There is a more direct way in which the crisis will affect work at the university and that is through the new understanding that teachers and students alike will bring to study based on their firsthand experience with revolution. Some find a previously held intellectual position with revolutionary implications no longer acceptable:

> I had been very involved in the LaFeber-Williams school of foreign policy and it is very critical of the capitalist system. [. . .] I realized that this sort of thing is the logical consequence of what we have been teaching. These kids are taking it seriously. They really believe it. And I wondered, "Do I really believe it?" Because I know that during that week I was pretty much against the revolution.
>
> I started to read all the economic history I could get ahold of. Before I say this again I want to make sure I know what I am talking about. I'm not convinced I'm right because I'm not willing to act upon it. Maybe there is a way to change the system within itself. [. . .] I am going to find it.

The revolution gave many, including men who were scholars in the field, their first personal experience with political and social upheaval and it made them realize that there were concepts they had used intellectually that had no existential meaning for them. Words like "revolution" and "legitimacy" took on new significance, which must reflect itself in teaching. The freshness of this moment, which showed how painfully large was the gap between academic and experiential learning, opened some to a new sensitivity to defects in their teaching. A young faculty member noted this change in himself:

> I have found myself as a teacher groping and being dissatisfied with the lecture method. It makes the students feel alienated—things are imposed from without and

they don't feel any sense of mastery [. . .]. I've been disappointed in coming back to Cornell to see very bright students groping for a method to change this.

Suddenly things are falling into place. The thing that struck me about this week was that the reason people were so exhilarated was because they were *doing* something for a change [. . .].

The way it is now, you assign all of your students approximately the same paper, and you're not really interested in reading it. You just want to get it out of the way. And you convey this to students—that they have nothing to tell you. At least the way I run a seminar, I would ask a question knowing the answer I wanted ahead of time. And people are trying to figure out, "What does he want?" and they fish for it. During this week students really knew more of what was going on than the teacher [. . .]. The SDS idea of participatory democracy is an ideal of self-extension that one can try to create in the classroom.

A graduate student of colonial history brought new understanding to the subject of his dissertation:

If there is anybody I identify with after all this, it's Governor Hutchinson. Hutchinson was a man of principle. Here he is faced with the cracking up of his society and people were nailing him for all kinds of things which he couldn't understand. His whole society was falling apart under him. I know how he felt.

Another graduate student felt that the subject of her thesis had taken form in a way that derived from the crisis experience:

In terms of my thesis, things have suddenly firmed up. My thesis is dealing with the development of Anglican apologetics, 1640–1660, during the war period. And I'm suddenly seeing the problems of authority and conscience much more clearly than I did before.

There were conversions and revelations, euphoria and despair. We and Cornell can no longer be the same.

This period of dramatic group formations and reformations was accompanied by a keen awareness of personal loss. Mixed in with the enthusiasm of rebirth and resurrection was the grief of personal deprivation and death. Death imagery recurred frequently throughout the week. Tom Jones sounded the keynote when he announced that "Cornell University has three hours to live." He cleverly (and I think quite accurately) carried through his thought by announcing after the faculty reversal on Wednesday that Cornell University—the old university run without recognition of student power—did die as he had predicted. At a teach-in on Friday afternoon a professor of history presented a eulogy for the university that had died. He began with the rabbinically intoned comment that the Talmud says that a Jew must mourn for the passing of the dead and he was fulfilling his religious obligation in memory of a cherished institution. The university had been the last institution where it was possible to live a decent, humane life and now, instead of running to protect their professors, students intimidated them into immoral submission and destroyed this last refuge. The graduate student dorm counselor, quoted earlier, reported the following dream which conveys her sense of entrapment in the responsibilities of caring for a dead institution:

I had the same nightmare for three successive nights. It was very vivid. Someone had died. It was a casual acquaintance, not someone I knew well. Not someone I had a real relationship with or felt any responsibility for. But other people were making me be responsible for this

dead person—for washing the corpse and getting it ready
for burial, and I was very angry at this.

It was not surprising that death was a preoccupation, for
the world was moving, and we were moving—some because
they wanted to and others because they had no choice. When
the revolution appeared successful a young professor felt, "It
was one of the saddest days of my life." The losses were on
both sides—the radicals mourned for their aborted revolution
and the faculty grieved for a lost way of life. Awake and
asleep, we struggled with our bereavement.

There were no buildings burned at Cornell that spring,
but there are ashes. It is tempting for me as a psychiatrist
to point to the organic cycle of growth and say, "Yes, there
was pain, but we have moved to something larger—the next
step." But as a historian I feel no such optimism. The boy
may move on to manhood through a trying adolescence, but
we have too many examples of revolutions that have created
evils more fearful than the institutions they set out to destroy.

THE UNIVERSITY IN TRANSITION

DAVID I. GROSSVOGEL

David I. Grossvogel was born in 1925. He is Goldwin Smith professor of comparative literature and romance studies and former chairman of the Humanities Council at Cornell. He has written as a drama critic and on literary theory. Among his major publications are *The Self-conscious Stage* (Columbia University Press, 1958); *Four Playwrights and a Postscript* (Cornell University Press, 1962); *Limits of the Novel* (Cornell University Press, 1968).

Perhaps we have gone beyond words. Or perhaps it is simply the acceleration of time—events move too fast and too erratically for the relative permanence of the recorded statement. It seemed possible, once, to pin the world down with words, to seize and define it. There was even a long and optimistic time when it seemed possible to change the world with words, to move through them as up the rungs of a ladder. But these days, modes and ideas have a short life span. And the idea of dialogue may well be no more than another figment of nostalgia—more dross on the slag pile of our yesterdays. Between nations, between people—the dogma of the deaf. The articulate possess the truth and can only assert; intransigence is the new morality, the only expression worthy of revelation. Dialogue demeans the absolute, convictions are non-negotiable. And there have long since been too many reasons to be suspicious of words: we know what fears they mask, what duplicities, what sexual convolutions. Amen. In which case this is merely catharsis. The slag pile may grow huge enough to bury us all, but we will die talking. Since we are being driven anyway to residual human utterances, that one will do as a starter.

Then, again, it is possible that words never changed anything. Maybe they were never more than a pastime of the idle—like that of the mandarins who sat before a censer into which scents had been blended in order to rediscover the original aromatics of the blend: a refined game for subtle but immobile people. Words used most exaltedly, "in the pursuit of truth," require leisure and a certain amount of well-being. And that "truth," even if it is occasionally glimpsed, seldom moves mountains. Truth is pursued within the privileged intervals of a routine but does not alter that routine which serves to preserve what has always been, including the appointed intervals during which truth is pursued.

There is, of course, no reason to believe that the new mandarins did not practice the ethics of the truth they sought. There is no reason to doubt that, to the extent that they were men moving amidst men, their encounters were generous and humane. It may have been a matter of temperament, but their wisdom also taught them that this kind of behavior is least abrasive and so best calculated to reduce the risk of man being an animal to man. And as a collective body, they were aware that the world is far from being perfect: they contributed their small perfectibility as a haven in the knowledge of the many imperfections that attempts at larger perfectibilities might likely engender. Or they simply offered their example as the slow but progressive way to wider perfectibility. In either case, those whose homeland was words seldom expected their words to achieve radical or instantaneous change. Possibly they envisaged no more than symbolic change—the kind of change that one might expect in a verbal world.

This left quite unmoved the ones whose condition did not

make this sort of pastime particularly attractive, because their circumstances had either not prepared them for it or failed to provide them with the leisure and the peace of mind to enjoy it. For these, the world could not remain a place where change was only symbolic or slow. When the leisurely meliorism of those who enjoyed leisure had dragged on too long, those who had run out of time sought non-symbolic change quickly, through physical action. Revolutions always catch the theorists by surprise (the non-revolutionary theorists, of course) and make them feel uncomfortable because they both confirm a part of their speculations and jeopardize the world in which speculation is possible.

And there has always been a third group, the largest by far: the managers of the world's affairs—men without a form of their own, shaped by whatever shapes most compellingly, dedicated to the elimination of what is defined for them as problems, accepting as virtue the virtual. The managers are concerned with neither precedents nor theory: theirs is a world of given facts that claim their attention entirely, ignoring the vision of the past or the agony of consequence. They are the doers. They are related to the verbal mandarins only inasmuch as they must perforce work within present structures. Revolutions surprise them too; they consider them hasty and unseemly arrogations of their own investiture. They resume their composure and their usual duties once the revolution has been successful.

Much like any community, Cornell sheltered all three points of view within its walls in April 1969—and also a revolution. But points of view do not constitute social classes or structural levels; they are only postures of the mind. One would, of course, expect a large segment of the faculty to live largely by words and within a universe of symbols. But there was also a sufficiency of other faculty members there to tell the first, "Oh, you people are far more interested in rehearsing the old problems than in doing anything about them." Nor did the students represent the constituency of a single point of view—in fact, they too were a microcosm of their society, ranging from those who thought that the world was their oyster to debate and examine to those who thought it was theirs to swallow whole and were preparing to do so. And by 1969, Cornell had also brought into its community another group for whom words or deeds within the existing structure had long been unsatisfactory: those among the blacks who had begun to experience throughout the world the beneficial effects of voicing anger pent up in them during centuries of economic and social bondage. Their attitude was ambiguous; Cornell's was simply naïve. Cornell assumed for them, as it had for the few blacks admitted previously, that access to the Establishment would be sufficient compensation. They had reckoned with only a part of the black's desire. They do not seem to have been aware that an emerging sense of racial cohesiveness would view such efforts as tokenism, or worse, as a tactical way of splitting off a privileged few from the concerns of the many. These blacks could live neither within a system that threatened to assimilate them nor without the gains, both socially symbolic and tangible, they were achieving through their show of strength.

These blacks were joined by a new breed, those who would have been, under normal circumstances, most sensitive to the exigencies of idealism and impatience but whose itch was exacerbated at this moment in American life by the boredom and sterility of suburbia—and, most likely, by parents who understood the good life primarily in terms of its goods (parents possibly frightened also by the popular pedagogy and infant management of their generation into substituting permissiveness for the values they lacked). These young whites of the upper bourgeoisie were less ambiguous than the blacks: caste privileges had given them whatever material good their society could offer, and having judged that society to be corrupt, they were able to call for its abolition without qualms. They became the unsolicited allies of the blacks. Their ranks were swelled further by a number of the faculty who thought exactly as they did—perhaps for the very same reasons (only the old have experienced more than youth —the young believe their state to be unique and permanent; it is not always easy for a student to understand that a teacher is a recent student, sometimes a very recent student—and, as likely as not, a student still).

Needless to say, Cornell was far from unique. Though in some ways a curious social entity, it was by and large a fairly representative microcosm; it certainly did not create any of the forces that it helped to set in motion, and the various collective voices heard on the campus did not belong to traditionally identifiable groups, black or white, student or faculty. The only corporate voice of the university was that of the administration. To say, as has been said since, that the administrative voice failed, leaving formulations to a divided faculty and an articulate minority of students, describes events but neglects their cause. The failure of the administrative voice in crisis was due in part to the clarity of its articulation before the crisis—and that which it articulated. And it too, though it spoke for Cornell, was but the echo of a greater affirmation.

President Perkins gave the Stafford Little lectures that compose *The University in Transition* in 1965. They are the words of one whose purpose is to identify and resolve the problems that the operative society posits as givens, and who has marked off, for a time, the university as the grounds for this operation. For him, the university is consequently defined by its "social involvement" (p. 32); he derides the "intellectual chastity" that would turn it into an aberrant or isolated part of the national scene were it not to reflect that evolving scene faithfully; he predicts in conclusion that "universities will have to modify their instincts for autonomy and take their places as full partners in [. . .] new planning agencies" (p. 86). He therefore deplores "increased attention to the traditional disciplines" (p. 4), believing instead that "the university has now come to the point where theory and doctrine must encounter the practical problems"

(p. 5). Here is quite obviously no mere man of words: "Knowledge acquired and transmitted must be used or it becomes sterile and inert" (p. 7), while "various of its parts are replaced as they become obsolete." Such a credo is, of course, close to the activist's, whose stated aim is to change, not to speculate about, what is wrong with the world. The part of *The University in Transition* that calls "for continuous change and innovation" (p. 80) in the name of "public service" is not so very different in its formulation, its aim, and its derivation, from the SDS pamphlet that urges abrogation of the existing university in order to bring an end to an unsatisfactory society. Both points of view represent, with variations, the legacy of a pragmatic people who believe that man's well-being can be achieved most effectively by changes in his physical environment.

Where the two points of view differ is not so much in their desire to change physical conditions in order to effect human betterment, but rather in the scope of the physical change that they envisage. Perkins is willing to effect these changes only in the university, so that it might fulfill its "responsibility for the integration of teaching, research and public service," since he believes (as does the SDS, by the way) that the university is an intimate partner and supporter of the society that spawned it:

> . . . the ideas and manpower of the university have helped turn government to an increasing preoccupation with public welfare, and they have helped give the profit-making corporation a far larger public orientation than it has ever had before. We should note again that this mixture of private pursuit and public purpose is hardly conceivable without the universities as partners, and this partnership would be impotent if the university had not come to embrace its complementary missions which have enabled it to digest new ideas, train new students, and participate in new applications (p. 19).

Perkins assumes that the industrial society is governed by forces that are more legitimately determining for society as a whole than are those that might evolve within the university were it to become isolated and distinct from that society. Here the SDS view differs: it believes, on the contrary, that the university is already too faithful a reflection of that society; and what Perkins wants to foster even more, it wants to eliminate altogether since it is convinced that both are indistinguishably corrupt. Where both views reveal a single birthplace is in the fact that neither is willing to allow the university a physiognomy, intellectual and value-oriented, that might be different from the rest of society's.

If allowed to proceed to its full flowering, Perkins' university would shun "the barren discussions of medieval scholasticism" (p. 9). Within the trinity of "teaching, research, and public service," research would develop into a special endeavor. It would no longer be a mere game, or mental bent, but something practical, a "search for the new" that shows "what could be rather than what is" (p. 7). Instead of concerning itself so burdensomely with "transmission of old knowledge" (p. 11), it would "establish relations with public and private authorities" (p. 12) so as not to remain a sectarian slave of the old. The German university of the nineteenth century failed, according to Perkins, because it did not establish such relations ("the missions of instruction and public service were neglected") and similarly, though Oxford and Cambridge "might be gracious," what is graciousness?—they are after all "not necessarily stimulating" and that is because they lack "interaction with English society" (p. 13). Graciousness belongs to a world of "general education" as opposed to modern society's requirements for "specialized" competency: "the responsibilities for general education have slowly been assumed by the high school and the preparatory school" (pp. 20–21); "For the student who wants to specialize [. . .] liberal education will have to be provided either by the secondary school or by a special program" (p. 44).

In accepting that the university should be closely wedded "to the world supporting that university" (p. 15), Perkins is aware, but does not flinch from the thought, that the university must become as dynamic and polymorphous as society itself. He is conscious of George Beadle's concern that university growth is out of hand: "Growth begets more growth, and specialization more specialization" (p. 23). And "as the relations between the university and other institutions of society proliferate" it becomes increasingly difficult for the university to determine its identity. Here too Perkins sees specialization as protection from dispersiveness: "Knowledge is growing so fast that no university can pretend to cover it all" (p. 34). There must therefore be "different programs to fit different institutions and different students" (p. 43). This is not only a clear indication of how little we can afford to be burdened with the lessons of the past, but acknowledgment that we no longer possess a common lore or human bond: there remain only the demands forced upon us by the dynamics of our society.

Caught up in the consequences of this involvement, the university becomes a monster requiring such huge expenditures that the usual sources of income are no longer equal to the need. Its sustenance "requires more and more hard-to-get books and [. . .] more and more airplane tickets" (p. 65). The monster turns into something less and less manageable and less and less distinct from its socio-political environment: "as cost and importance of educational matters increase, decision-making moves up the hierarchical scale, and away from the educational institutions toward political structures" (p. 84). Perkins counsels ultimately that since you can't fight 'em, join 'em; public and private regulatory agencies already operative within our society, the government and foundations, may well be the new "national planners" (p. 72), but they will be infected with his educational optimism as "the university [becomes] only one level in the whole vast hierarchy of education that has been built up around it" (p. 77). With the loss of autonomy and with the idea of "public service" achieving the ultimate ingestion of the university by an industrial society, a comprehensive rationale for universities has been reached—a twentieth-century updating (through our own special know-how) of something like the French university complex (against whose centralization French students only recently undertook a revolution of their own, attempting among other things a return to local autonomies).

For all that Perkins intends to be "provocative" and "useful" (p. vii), his thesis is largely that on which the majority of American universities has long rested—the Rousseau-like vision of a public-minded education relying heavily on the acquisition of technical skills, which Perkins traces back to the ideals of Franklin and Jefferson. And certainly this was the sort of practical vision that led Ezra Cornell to found *his* institution—a not unlikely place toward which those disenfranchised during three centuries might turn for the tools and the traits with which to claim quickly (and with more than merely the force of moral right) the socio-economic benefits that are the self-justification of our consumer society. And very likely, it is from the university's eighteenth-century ideal of a socially conscious pragmatism that today's SDS leader learned to be dissatisfied with the consequences of that ideal—since an ideal of service to society does not necessarily condone the military-industrial complex fostered by that society.

When Perkins talks about "education that opens doors to the good life" (p. 24) one must infer from his context what that "good life" is. It clearly stems from, and centers around, the notion of an enlightened pragmatism. But that ideal adumbrates through its disclaimers the suggestion of another need. Perkins keeps waving away a persistent and nagging fly: "After all, a liberal education is the objective of a lifetime. Why assume that it should be crowded into the first two post-secondary years?" (p. 44). But the fact is that

Perkins doesn't know quite where to crowd it. Quite likely out of the university altogether: "the responsibilities for general education have slowly been assumed by the high school and the preparatory school" (pp. 20–21). Or perhaps there might subsist small liberal arts colleges, like commemorative stelae upon the industrial landscape ("faculty-student relationship [. . .] can best be found in an independent liberal arts college, a fruitless search that adds to the problem of internal cohesion in the university" [p. 45]).

And so the paradox of non-relevancy is born within a university that tries to be totally relevant. Perkins could not know at the time he was propounding these ideals that within a few short years six thousand of his own students would assemble, as they were doing on many other campuses, to reject his vison of the good life. The idea of a partnership between the university and society at a time when that society is being called into question is doubly ironic because it not only opens the university to a charge of guilt through association but robs the university of what should be its natural role as the critic of society or, in the fields of practical endeavor, of at least its posture of independence from society. But the truth is, of course, that the university was open to such charges long before *The University in Transition* was even conceived. It was generally a place that dealt in facts rather than values, in quantities rather than qualities.[1] The inadequately represented part of the university that attempted to resist this norm was usually considered useless by those who dealt in tangibles or subversive by those whose ideas required the security of the social matrix in which they were shaped. And so the university remained largely a composite of praxis and prestige, preparing its students for positions of maintenance within society and an espousal of its traditional values. The university did produce an occasional mutant, and loosed upon society the lone voice of a writer who did

[1] Among the most distinguished voices raised during the crisis in support of Perkins were those of Cornell scientists.

not write in order to sell, a philosopher who dealt in heresies, an artist who shunned modes: they were something less than a threat to society—in fact they came in such small numbers as to be scarcely audible. They were the few who had brooded in a history or a literature seminar over the dilemma of the human condition and the pathetically inadequate ways in which man attempts to overcome it, or who had glimpsed, within a poem or a telescope, more satisfactory harmonies.

The apparent paradox (for it is only apparent) is why the dissatisfaction of so few should have suddenly spread to so many. It would be tempting to infer that traditionally soul-narrowing universities were simply too boring for words. But that is unfortunately not the whole truth. Not even a significant part of it. The forces of change came, not as they should have, from within the university, but from without. At Cornell as elsewhere, the pre-professionals, whether in fraternities or applied methodologies, endured the turmoil in silence or resentment; most had not questioned their world until then, and many were not prepared to have others question it when the time for questions came. At best they went through the negative catharsis of racial guilt—a very small part of the human dilemma. The "education that opens doors to the good life" had failed them. But it had failed others as well. Those prepared by means, leisure, and a conscience to criticize and conceive reasoned change had been equally short-changed. Bereft of fundamental meanings and imaginative vision, they could only assert their frustration and their anger. They had few viable alternatives to formulate and were left to express that failure through the exhilaration but ultimate sterility of nay-saying. A better life, within society or the self, requires harder thinking.

And so, quite possibly, we may have been carried permanently beyond words. If the dynamics of change failed to originate within the mind and soul of the university, if they are now free of rational control, if they have become their own motor propulsion, we are rudderless, outward bound toward new galaxies; and human terms, as we knew them, have lost their meaning. The instant changes required by the harshest critics of an industrial society become no more than a reflection of the self-sustaining need for change within the commercial sector of that society. But in the old human terms, within the university, we missed an opportunity.

For the playboy and pre-professional university of the past, the infusion of a new force—the black—might once have represented rebirth. It would have helped to shatter the sterile structures of elitism, vitalized the student body with an element desperately hungry to know and far richer than most in the kind of stored-up agony out of which awareness of self and others starts. An understanding of black culture, black history, the suffering and the songs born of them, the insights, would have swelled measurably the ever under-nourished humanities that grope as painfully as a late summer stream across the parched lands of the practical university. The black would have been a gainer—but only to the extent that the university would have gained, through the assertion of its most legitimate and most difficult quest: the investigation of the human quandary. But, of course, that sort of research achieves no quantitative results, though it might help to pro-mote a better kind of revolution. In the good old days, when there was no threat to worry about, such concerns were marginal to the traditional university. However, once a revolt broke traditional dams, it was sorrily a thing of this starvation, the vision of a stunted sight. It rose in anger against the old forms, but posited its aims largely within the limitation of those old forms or in the merely destructive terms of that anger—what Camus called a rebellion—as opposed to a gen-uine revolution.

Alongside those who, through shortsightedness, want to rearrange the same old pieces into a new pattern without reflecting on the consequences of such circular thinking are those who do not even seem to know quite what they might do with the stray pieces. Mingled in proportions that are difficult to distinguish are their feelings of resentment, impatience, desire, and contempt. Their way of coming to terms with the objects of these confused feelings is to destroy those objects. Within the university, they are the ones who want to paralyze it and bring it to its knees, with only vague expressions about what might come subsequently. Though somewhat inarticulate on construction, they are articulate, skilled, and purposeful in keeping the tenants of the old order off balance and ineffectual, tangling them up in their feelings of guilt and do-goodism, or alternately acting as the tide of history and inviting the traditional realists to accept the inevitable. And those who have always been quick to recognize what is because they have never been quite sure about what ought to be are sensitive to this kind of evidence.

Activists may be myopic in the sight of history when they claim only the short-term benefits of their destructive action —a sense of purpose, unity, and self-awareness. But these at least they achieve, and they remain unencumbered by theory or the consequent hypocrisy of having to face up to its results. The others, those who invoke a future morality for their action, make a weaker case for that action in proportion as they corrupt the immediacy of a self-generating purpose with abstract diagnoses. It is easy enough to verify that the built-in mechanism for change was not working either well enough or quickly enough to alter the old university from a society-shaped to a society-defining body; and manifestly, a show of force brought about instantaneously, and through illegitimate means, a number of legitimate departures that would have required years of talk to achieve. Cornell has now funded and begun a black studies program; departments that may have been reluctant to enter into a dialogue with their students now do so more freely; a Constituent Assembly has proposed a new university senate supposedly seeking better ways to shape the university structure. But the fundamental questions are whether the black studies program will be more than a mere expediency; whether dialogue within present departments can be fruitful (whether the present form of departments is in fact justified); and whether the new senate can bring out of the past a scheme for the future. Criticism is not the sum total of human wisdom.

The difficulty begins with an adequate definition of the good life. If the university is to provide basic answers, it must surely look beyond mere techniques or patchwork. When Perkins suggests "different programs to fit different institutions and different students" he displaces a more general ideal—"to embrace certain values, such as intellectual honesty, tolerance, and the capacity for wise judgment" (p. 43)—for he goes on to urge "a reexamination" of the extent to which the university can cope with a "liberal education," since the university cannot devote its main concerns to the fostering of human values when its primary responsibility is to the specialized demands of a technological society. His university thus acquires a solipsistic morality and definition:

> University integrity, then, is involved not with preserving things as they are, but rather with maintaining the coherence of its various parts, and the harmony with which it is able to pursue its aims—whatever their specialized nature (p. 33).

> It is also true that expert advice can be found most frequently and in greater variety in the university than in any other institution; indeed, hardly any field of knowledge in the university has not felt the heady experience of being publicly useful (p. 37).

These are hardly fundamental definitions of the university since they would define as well the special virtues of the trade school, the industrial lab, or the paid consultant. Expert advice based on research is neither the most meaningful nor the most exclusive service that the university can provide. Its special contribution is the self-awareness and the human values it can foster *even* through the most specialized kind of impersonal research. And it is because the humanities are traditionally concerned with these values in their most immediate statement (literature, philosophy, history, the arts, etc.), and their research (an exercise that does not necessarily turn a man toward the future, but can as easily turn him toward the past, and should certainly always return him to his most inward self) that the university malaise begins, not only at Cornell, within the arts and humanities.

To limit oneself to a general statement about "human values" avoids the problem without even defining it. Human values voiced by the ghetto militant and the affluent activist may sound alike, but their very genesis makes them different. The experience of hunger and social ostracism will define values according to socio-economic terms with greater human acuity than will social reaction to an affluent society that possessed already all of the goods (and some of the good) that the underprivileged require—and most likely more. But a university cannot promote physical change; it can promote only spiritual change. It takes over whenever technologies have done their best for man and there remains the soul to cope with. Once the hungry have been fed, there remains yet another hunger: men still leap off bridges even after they have become bank presidents. As distinct from the trade school or the industrial lab, the university should concern itself not with what changes but with the staples by which man lives—the need and nature of truth, the imposition of moral values upon the animal, the pursuit and the pleasure of the aesthetic.

It is at this point that we run out of words. So much has been written already, and to what purpose? There has been so much conviction, so little convincing. . . . The idealist who rejects in his puritanism even such rudimentary terms as the good, the true, and the beautiful because they are the terms or the spawnings of a corrupt society is likely to accuse those for whom the words have meaning of being ivory-tower cultists insensitive to the plight of that society's victims. Such intransigence discourages dialogue. One is reduced to affirmations: the terms themselves may well be meaningless or relative, but beyond the capriciousness of fashions and the casuistry of definitions, they state a human constant and a human need. One can only assert the validity of that need and reject the accusation that questions its legitimacy. The society that is supposed to have nurtured this ivory-tower indulgence never really did. A businessman is not likely to look with more favor on faculty privilege than the most radical of student nay-sayers. Further, the very voice of student dissent argues against its own nihilism: however incensed with society, it did not wait to get out into the mainstream of that society to find its political forum. This implies at least minimal affinities between that voice and the classroom's, and suggests that a sympathetic echo is more likely on the campus than on the city street. And, though it is true that the woods are burning and we must, if we are to survive at all, look to the causes of the fire (a fire that would most likely not have started as readily had human values not been held in contempt by so many arsonists), it follows nevertheless that an understanding of its causes requires wisdom and experience if we are not to repeat the old mistakes too quickly. More important, when the fire is out and the woods are replanted, will they be worth living in if we have not somehow been able to sustain a consciousness of what is true, good, and beautiful?

The university should be the place that preserves this memory and offers each a chance to return in his own way to its sustenance. It should posit a man at the center of all of its concerns, however narrow that concern, or esoteric. The university would be well advised to put the ROTC and all recruiting beyond its walls, not simply in response to the requests of radical students, but because such encumbrances come between the university and its purpose. It should teach its students how to remain unique in a stultifying collectivity, how to preserve peace and dignity in the midst of the huge forces that must be set in motion to meet even the most rudimentary demands of the many. It should teach its students how to remain a witness and a conscience in the world beyond the university when the temptation to do so begins to weaken in proportion as results come less readily, encounter more hostility and require a lifetime of possibly solitary stubbornness.

In the old university, the inadequate humanities were the special province of these concerns. But they were further enfeebled in proportion as any other part of the campus could forget that they were at the center of that campus and at the center of its own concerns no matter how distant these might appear to be. It is difficult to disagree with the extremists who objected to a faculty concerned with an amoral, apersonal research that had become deaf to its human echo.

Still, one fails to see what is to be gained from abolishing the good in order to root out the evil. Nay-saying can become another kind of self-indulgence that soon dissipates its first gains. The disappearance of reason and the promotion of superficial reasons are equally destructive. Of what use is the bucolic naïveté of those who believe that even in the best of worlds one might endow with a private morality the industrial monster that is required to feed, shelter, and clothe such vast numbers? Our neo-primitives wear beads and wire-rimmed glasses mass-produced by an industry that they promoted. Those who chase out the Chase recruiters are doing so on scholarships paid for with dirty money simply because there is no such thing as clean money. It is a matter of numbers and needs—and those numbers and needs will be with us in the most perfect society. What one might do, however, is to curb the population explosion, so that there will be enough food and air to go around. And then concentrate on values rather than on possessions so that the demented growth of the industrial monster can be brought within bounds. Saving society will be a sterile exercise if we cannot decrease air pollution, preserve some clear water, perhaps a few trees, and a little human space where a man can escape for a while from the blessings of collectivization. The mechanistic idealists of the right and the left ought to give some thought to what comes after they have attained their mechanistic Eden. And then consider that more and more are doomed to become creatures of leisure in this technological world and that leisure requires training for survival: remember the American custom of dropping dead upon retirement.

Slogans are an inadequate substitute for an appraisal of the human condition. So are anger and instant wisdom. In May 1968, during the Paris version of our own academic turmoil, a poster on one of the Sorbonne walls urged the militants to become hard in order to preserve human tenderness. It was a quotation from Che Guevara. A revolution that is aware of its human limitations seems hopeful to me. But then, the French may have had a bad university, but they have had a long experience of what is necessary to make life livable. I came away with a different feeling, in July 1969, two months after our own turmoil, after seeing a seven-fifteen local showing of Pontecorvo's *Battle of Algiers* —a picture of people caught in the vicious spiral of violence and counterviolence through which the most legitimate revolution is robbed of its purpose. The SDS had assumed retrospective sponsorship of the evening, canceling a planned meeting in order to encourage its members' attendance. They filled most of the seats when I was there, handed out their literature, spoke from the stage before the show began. When the first French policeman was shot on the screen, small exclamations of approval broke out. And as the fiction on screen began to develop its moral lesson, these socially conscious spectators began enacting the failure portrayed. With each NFL killing, the shouts of approval grew louder. At the height of the picture, as a car drives down the main street of Algiers machine-gunning passers-by at random, the audience was convulsed in an orgy of jubilant anger. These were supposedly our best students—the ones most sensitive to the needs and dilemmas of our times, the ones in whom our hope for a more humane world is vested. That is what comes from the humanistic impoverishment of a university.

Where do we turn from here? The abdication of the mind, the giving up of words bodes no good for the future. An administration sensitive to the public opinion of an industrial society cannot do very much more than respond with material concessions to ill-formulated demands. The process is circular and sterile. The traditional liberals among faculty and students, themselves the products of inchoate thought, are helpless to articulate convictions that they can trust. Only within a culture that has put so little time into its concern for the human quandary can the liberal mind consent to be paralyzed by black accusations that the white cannot understand the black simply because he is white. Only the intellectually insecure within any society can accept the argument that the humanities, supported by a repressive society, are an opiate devised by that society. It takes a tougher mind, more deeply immersed in the private world of man, to answer that no human problem is alien to any man and that those entrusted with this lesson failed, not because they were sustained by a corrupt society, but because that society never considered them to be particularly interesting or central. Perkins himself acknowledges that our society encourages, through its one-sided sponsorship, that which he terms "the breach between C. P. Snow's two worlds" (p. 22). The truth is, however, that there have never been two worlds as Snow defines them—unless one accepts that man is an aggregate of universal and tangible parts that can be analyzed exactly, classified with precision, and categorically saved. But it is only the unessential part of man that can be so defined, and all matter, whether book or biological datum, is inert until a human sensitivity beholds it. And it is this sensitivity that ultimately renders trivial Snow's explanation of the two cultures. There are not two cultures, the scientific and the humanistic; there are only two kinds of scientists, just as there are two kinds of humanists: the humanistic and the non-humanistic scientist; the humanistic and the non-humanistic humanist. If the work of the scientist and that of the humanist is concerned with the awareness of human possibilities, through the awareness of all that man has ever attempted and the record of his frustrations; if its purpose is to rehearse the human condition out of a sense of the extent to which man must continue to fail and a sense of how unacceptable such failure is; if its purpose is to experience how exalting and how ultimately trivial are man's most shining victories, then that work, whether scientific or not, is humanistic.

It is the pragmatists, both the denigrators and the apologists of society, who starve the human spirit by looking for salvation in a world of objects, for change in a world of deeds. The radical activists and the managerial types run along the same treadmill, unaware of, or indifferent to, the fact that no accomplishment is greater than man's ability to contemplate it and that, perhaps, the only enduring form of his world is in the words of his reflection upon it. Perhaps, when all is said and done, "the barren discussions of medieval scholasticism" were ultimately less barren than the quest "for continuous change and innovation": the first were able at least to attain their enjoyment. Words and reflections may not be substantial, but they nourish better and longer than do gadgets and gadgetry—and because they are their own reward, they are less likely to engender frustratingly inaccurate prophets.

PART II

FOREWORD

The article that follows was written with the black community in mind. It seeks to contribute substantially to our understanding of the assumptions and strategies of black students on a white campus and the university obstacles these assumptions and strategies were intended to anticipate and overcome. To facilitate this understanding, the essay attempts to answer the question of why black students occupied Willard Straight Hall by analyzing black students' perceptions of conditions at Cornell and relating these perceptions to social situations within the Cornell black community and between that community and the larger white society. I have chosen to see the seizure of Willard Straight Hall as a product of black students' perceptions of Cornell University as an institution hostile to the interests of the black community, hostility which they saw symbolized in the treatment accorded black women on campus. The *presence* of black women led to the occupation of Willard Straight Hall.

But more importantly, the Willard Straight Hall incident suggests that black students' perceptions were in irrepressible conflict with other sets of perceptions—the university administration's, the white student body's, and the faculty's. This essay offers an interpretation of the administration's perception of black students in their relationship with the white community, but it does not adequately relate this perception to the administration's position within that community, especially its relationship with faculty members. Moreover, if there is any glaring omission in this book, it is the failure of any of the writers, including myself, to discuss the faculty's perception of black students and to understand this perception within the framework of the faculty's social and ideological positions. In another essay, I have tried to demonstrate that the Willard Straight Hall event brought to the surface long-suppressed feuds between individual faculty members, between ideological differences within the various schools and departments, and between the faculty, the university administration, and the growing number of radical white students. Willard Straight Hall revealed the impotence of the Cornell faculty, an impotence brought on, not by the overwhelming power of black students, but by its inability to provide a unified front and to act in a constructive and principled manner when confronted by a crisis.

This article leaves much unsaid. I hope that the black community will consider what has been written, compare it with other experiences we have shared as an oppressed people, and construct an ideology that will contribute to our development as a nation. We have spent much of our time analyzing liberal, conservative, and Marxist interpretations of our predicament. Having rejected them, we must develop a perspective that will explain who and what we are, and where we ought to move. If there is any misgiving for what happened at Cornell, it is that we were often inconsistent in dealing with the white community and ourselves, mainly because we have not become completely extricated from the values of white society. Perhaps discussions and criticisms of this article will serve as a starting point for a greater understanding of what is needed to resolve these difficulties.

C.D.

CORNELL: CONFRONTATION IN BLACK AND WHITE

CLEVELAND DONALD, JR.

Cleveland Donald, Jr., was born in 1946. He is a graduate student in Latin American history and a teaching assistant in Professor Andrew Hacker's "Politics and Society." Since graduating from the University of Mississippi, he has spent a summer in Brazil studying slavery and its abolition in Brazilian history. He is the recipient of a Ford Foundation Fellowship and plans to teach at a black college, while participating in community organizing within his native state.

Karl Mannheim in *Ideology and Utopia* develops the notion that the ideology of a particular group grows from the social situation of the group. The tensions within the group and within individual members derive from a clash of conflicting or opposing ideologies and occur generally among groups and individuals who are socially mobile—those who are confronted with conflicting life styles. At Cornell University the frustration of black students came from the independent action and interaction of two sets of conflicts. The first set occurred between the white institution and the black community, that is, between a white life style and a black life style. The second set occurred within the group and within individual members of the group. The first set of conflicts necessitated the occupation of Willard Straight Hall. The second set defined the process by which blacks finally decided that such strong measures were required.

It is difficult to observe a common denominator for the variety of blacks who attend Cornell University. Most of the black students at Cornell reside in the ghetto. A few of them do not. Some come from families that earn a comfortable income, while others come from families that struggle to survive. Some have received education at ghetto schools, and others have been educated at prep schools. But without exception and regardless of geographic location or economic income, most black students came to Cornell because of the greater mobility they would have within white society.

The major motive for the black student's desire for greater mobility is escape from the black community. Because of the racist nature of his earlier education, the black student generally has a negative image of his community. By the time the black student arrives at Cornell, the process of alienation from the black community has begun. Thus escape from the ghetto becomes a rejection of tenement flats with eight children and no father. However, because he has not yet lost the deeper sense of love of family and community, there may be a duality in his attitude toward the black community. The black student may accept the escape as an outright refusal to identify with the black community. At Cornell it is exemplified by those few students who have nothing whatsoever to do with most of the other blacks on campus. For the vast majority of the black students, the escape is perceived as a positive contribution to the improvement of the black community and is shrouded in the complex but sincere rationalization that the general uplift and improvement of the black community can best occur through the individual efforts of those members whose lives become a tribute to the race. In the latter instance, the black community, that is, the part with which the student is familiar, such as family and friends, encourages the student to escape, assuming that it is indeed the only alternative, given the limitation placed on black self-expression, for the uplifting of the black people.

Indirectly, the liberal paternalism of the Cornell white community inadvertently retards the process of escape and forces a common identity upon black students. Figuratively, every black student at Cornell, whether he lives there or not, lives within the shadow of the ghetto. In one sense, the ghetto is analogous to the plantation, and as the concept slave defined the status of blacks on the plantation, so the term COSEP (special program for bringing black students to Cornell) defines the status of black students at Cornell University. Whenever a white student encounters a black student, and indeed whenever one black meets another, it is assumed a priori that he participates in the COSEP program and that he comes from the ghetto.

Unlike the status slave on the plantation, the status COSEP and ghettoite at Cornell apparently has more advantage. For one thing, there is more money. For another, the black student is encouraged to conform to the stereotype of the ghetto life. This allows the student to add new dimensions to the narrow role he has played as high school intellectual. Ultimately the performing of other roles that are identified as characteristic of the ghetto makes the black student receptive to some deeper understanding of his community and its problems.

Neither the enthusiastic endorsement of whites nor the latent altruistic motivation of the black students themselves was sufficient to bring about the confrontation of April 23. In fact, a delicate balance existed in such a way as to allow the optimum co-optation of the black student. Sanctioned by whites, the black could finish four years at Cornell with only the trappings of ideology that would be beneficial to the black struggle. At graduation and upon re-entering a black world, if indeed he felt motivated to do so, he would have discovered a void in the development of his blackness that actually would have made him irrelevant to the black people.

The point should be emphasized: the university is a laboratory where an experiment in black-white relations is being performed to bring about greater social control of the black community, or at least a particular segment of that community. Given ideal conditions, and if it were possible to isolate the university as some academics claim, the experiment would be carried out with predictability and according to plan. But, like the impact of the African Independence Movement on the Afro-American experience, the rise of black nationalism within the black community intruded into the Cornell laboratory. In 1966, Stokely Carmichael marched through Mississippi and the echo of black power and its demands for immediacy terminated another period of peaceful co-existence in black-white relations.

The reverberations of black nationalism came to Cornell in two ways. Before the Meredith march, one generation of COSEP students had spent one year at Cornell, and the second generation was to enter in the fall. In the fall, following the march through Mississippi, white students called upon the first generation, whom all along they considered experts on the black community, to explain the new phenomenon. In explaining the new cry from the black community, this generation had to deal once more with the true effect of Cornell University upon their lives. When they had returned home during the summer, they had already had to deal with the changed mood of their community. Most importantly, they had to reassess their roles given the new demands of the black community. These demands raised the old contradictions in the apparent inconsistency between their aspiration and the needs of the community. The second generation, which came in the fall, had not been a party to the social contract that existed between whites and the black first generation. Having less of a need to justify the modus vivendi, since they had not constructed it, and arriving newly from the black community, this generation stridently attacked the whites and the black first generation for the racial situation on the campus. In the process they legitimated themselves as the oracles of black power on the predominantly white college campus. Whites turned to them, and this challenged the pre-eminent influence of the first generation.

The challenge to the first generation's authority as experts on the black community in white eyes was minor compared with the challenge to their influence over the black woman. In the original social contract between whites and the black first generation, the black woman had occupied a nebulous, undefined position. The typical black woman arriving at Cornell was innocent sexually. But since college has a liberating influence on sex attitude, she should have made certain changes in her sexual behavior. However, several factors prevented the black woman from dealing creatively with the question of sex. Because of the social myths associated with her color, she was considered loose and immoral. Particularly, the black sister suffered from the stereotype, with its stigma in white eyes, that every black woman will be an unwed mother. Her suffering came not from the fact that she considered an unwed mother morally reprehensible, but that it meant the end of her upward mobility, her major reason for being at Cornell. Usually her own family was upwardly mobile or was concerned about her mobility. With Victorian rhetoric her parents had already warned her that to get a good man she must get a good education, that black men were no good, that above all she had to be independent and able to fend for herself. In one sense, such an attitude contributed to the alienation of black women from black men.

If she had been the only female available, the black woman could have controlled the black man by holding over him the promise but not the actuality of sex. But at Cornell white women offered black men an alternative to black women. The black man said that he was attracted to the white woman partly because a relationship with her appeared to be less complicated than one with a black woman, since neither party initially contemplated that their relationship might lead to marriage.

In reality, by not allowing him to develop a relationship with a black woman, however complicated that relationship might have been, interracial dating restricted the maturation of the black man's personality and limited his ability to understand himself.

Often the black man-white woman relationship forced the black woman to make premature decisions concerning her relationship with black men. Frequently it relieved the black woman from having to deal with black men by providing her with the convenient rationalization that her predicament was primarily the fault of black men or white women. This attitude appeared in the justification put forward by some black women at Cornell that most of the marriages between black women and white men, which occur as often as those between black men and white women, if not more often, were due to the shortcomings of black men. They argued that every sister who married a white man had had a miserable experience with a black man. In all instances, whatever the rationale, the tensions between black men and women increased, inevitably affecting their perception of themselves and the black community.

Before the advent of black power, the black woman's life on campus was degrading and frustrating. In her own mind, the only possible justification for dating white men had to be marriage—not sex. In addition, it had to be directly related to some real and unpleasant affair with a black man. Whenever she did date interracially, the black coed had to endure the vigorous condemnation of the black male, who did not hesitate to apply the double standard. On the other hand, her childhood education, provided by the racists' society and reinforced by her perceived experience with black men, argued for the essentially negative concept of the black male.

The black woman developed two solutions to her problems. She dated only light-complexioned black males. As one dark-complexioned male reported, before black power, a dark-complexioned brother could not get a date or a dance

with a black woman. Or the black woman was attracted to
the black men whom white women found attractive. Both
approaches to the dilemma reflected the inner tensions of an
upwardly mobile individual who felt that she had to reject
her own culture and accept the dominant values of society
in order to succeed. Such a rejection was suicidal, for it
generated self-degradation and self-hatred.

Black power, or more precisely black nationalism, sought
to redefine and expand the traditional concept of manhood
in such a manner that it took into account the realistic condition of a black community. In the process it reaffirmed the
old idea that the black man could be understood best by con-
trasting him physically and emotionally with black women.
Furthermore, the new ideology incorporated the former understanding that authentication of one's manhood depended not
only on a personal recognition of its validity but on its acceptance by other men and especially women.

Manhood as expressed in the black nationalism that came
to Cornell said, "We must protect our women; we must love
our women." Love and protection of women became synony-
mous with the acceptance of oneself and of the black community. Other men, specifically white male students on the
campus, had to show their acceptance of the new definition
of the new black manhood by respecting the black women.
The black man had to reject white women. Although inclined
to be independent, even distrustful, black women accepted
the ideology and the self-subordination it required because
it brought them to center stage, focusing attention on them.
The black woman rewarded the philosophy's exponents by
showering them with attention. The first generation of black
Cornellians, that is, those whose members professed a genuine
concern for the black community, had to consider this new
outlook because it came from the black community and because the new generation of blacks was using it to challenge
the first's influence within the Cornell community.

Black nationalism also drew black men and women together

by removing much of the stigma attached to premarital sex. Prior to black power, a black woman who engaged in premarital sex was thought to have relinquished her principal weapon for attracting black men. Moreover the rejection of sex before marriage provided another opportunity to escape the black community, for ghettoites were reputed to be sexually loose. Black power said that sex was important as a cultural function rather than as a biological one, and it maintained that blacks were better at it than whites. The romanticizing of the ghetto, inherent in black power, brought respect to some of its activities—in this case, its reputed sexual habits. At the theoretical level, meaningful premarital sexual intercourse became a legitimate expression of one's humanity and one's blackness. Practically, it made women more open to sex, particularly since black power also assured them of the love and protection of black men. It also destroyed the basic rationale that black men had presented for dating white women.

The advent of black power coincided with and grew out of the failure of this country to fulfill Martin Luther King's dream. Before black power idealistic reformers had been critical of the society, but implicit in their actions was the belief that the society would correct its own inequities. The failure of integration, which was supposed to be society's way of self-preservation, spawned black power. Black power grew because, despite civil rights laws, the condition of the average black man worsened. It tried to give the black man a modicum of control over his own fate and attempted to prevent the total psychological emasculation of the black race. While the new ideology continued to blame society for the condition of black people, it maintained that black people themselves, not society, would be their own salvation. Under the new order, the black man retained his pride since he had ultimate control over his fate.

Attributing to an individual ultimate but not immediate control over his fate encourages introspection and self-criticism since the inevitable question, "Why wait?" raises itself. With proper supervision, this introspection is absolutely necessary to understanding the black community and self-actualization. But black students on white campuses like Cornell find it difficult to develop a critical self-analysis because, observed by whites, they feel the need to manifest a continuous display of unity. Nevertheless, when a group has separated itself from the dominant society, factions do develop which affect its ability to function. After black students at Cornell had developed a separate identity, for the reasons and through the process described above, the old and simple division between first and second generation gave way to three extremely complex factions which exhibited more intricate variations of the tendencies developed in the simpler division. The success of the Afro-American Society in dealing with the problems posed by factionalization did not come without struggle and conflict. Since the occupation of Willard Straight Hall occurred after a long period of developing internal consensus and unity within the Cornell black community, the process itself must be examined to understand the implications of the events of April 21 for black students.

By September 1968 three factions within the Cornell University Afro-American Society had reached their most perfect development: the Yippies, the Converts, the Radicals. The Yippies, as the Radicals labeled them, were artistic and "super cool." In their practice and philosophy one finds the notion of black people as a loving people given its most extreme expression. They resisted the constant preoccupation of the other factions with the white devils by asking black students to forget the honkey and to concentrate on love and respect within the black community. The implication of their philosophy meant withdrawal from the politics of dealing with white society and the development of strong interpersonal relationships among black students. The group's members, most of whom came from first-generation COSEP students, were known to date white women, although they managed to evade detection. They enjoyed the notorious reputation of being both heartbreakers and able to date any black woman they desired. The Yippies lived their philosophy and rarely involved themselves as a group or as individuals in the contest for power.

Narupa,[1] the leader of the Yippies, was a prep school product. Like most of the prep school students in the program, he had great difficulty in accepting the practical implications of militant black power. By September 1968, Narupa, as original founder and the second elected president of the Cornell Afro-American Society (1966–67), had become disenchanted with the political development of black students and frustrated with his incapacity to understand his own political role. A promising young writer, Narupa now served as editor of *Watu,* the black literary magazine. But his frustrations affected his ability to write and even to function well as editor of *Watu.* His dilemma was probably compounded by the thought that black people were as angry with him as he was with himself.

The typical Convert was also from the first generation, and middle class both mentally and economically. The failure of the fraternity system to accept him pushed him initially toward more radical expressions of concern for the black community and black separatism. After conversion to black separatism, Converts stopped interracial dating and through their political activism gained the allegiance of many of the black women. The Converts had close ties with the Yippies and a few of them, except for their political involvement, were actually a part of that group.

Any attempt to describe the Converts poses certain difficulties. One should not refer to them as moderates, for that would make the Yippies appear more conservative and the Radicals more radical. In fact, the Converts exhibited a political naïveté far more rudimentary than the complex

[1] These are assumed names that were sometimes used in actuality. —Eds.

Yippie philosophy. On occasion they would vehemently give the university fifteen minutes to live. At other times they would observe that whites could be trusted, a reactionary notion within the organization, and looked disappointed and angry when white liberals did not do what they had expected of them. I have called them Converts, but they were charter members of the Afro-American Society. Yet, until the attempted fraternity boycott in the late fall of 1966, they had infrequently attended meetings. The Converts try harder, but their earnest political concern often far outdistanced their political grasp of the cause. One could interpret the Yippies' emphasis on love rather than politics as "unpolitical" and consequently either conservative or radical because it went beyond politics. But the Yippies at least had a program distinctively different from the Radicals'. The Converts and Radicals sometimes said the same things but with competing and conflicting meanings. Because they had chosen the political avenue to relevancy, the Converts rather than the Yippies offered the real challenge to the Radicals.

Prior to the attempted fraternity boycott mentioned above, black students saw little need to organize as an activist group. The Afro-American Society was founded as an integrated body "to foster cultural exchange among as many different groups as exist in our community and to undertake any program or projects that furthers knowledge of the significant contributions of black America." Nowhere did its constitution state that the body would attempt to aid the struggle of black people or even to improve the life of a black student on campus.

The second academic year for the Society began with the defense of black power. The major expression of the members' thoughts on the new ideology was printed in the *Cornell Daily Sun* supplement, October 21, 1966, called "Black Power—Its Implication." One article written by a first-generation black, entitled "The Thread of Mighty Armies," told whites to work in their own neighborhood and defined black power as "a removal of the heretofore all-white power structure and a redistribution of this power to all Americans, more specifically, the Afro-Americans and the Spanish Americans and especially the coming together and organization of all black Americans to form a position of unified strength." Another article said that racial unity added "needed momentum to the over-all racial situation." Clearly the rationale for separation was accepted by black students. They lacked only the opportunity to give it practical expression.

On October 22, 1966, Phi Delta Theta held a dance which featured the Rocketts, a local black band. The affair drew many people from the town as well as those on campus. Following the dance, Narupa, a member of the Interfraternity Council's Discrimination Committee, reported that black students had been charged a dollar admission while whites had not. The Discrimination Committee recommended to the IFC Judiciary Board that it look into the matter. After its investigation, the Judiciary issued a ruling, subsequently upheld by the Faculty Review Board, which placed the house on social probation for the remainder of the academic year.

Phi Delta Theta argued that the admission fee had been charged to Ithacans to prevent them from overcrowding the party. The Judiciary stated its belief that "the policy of Phi Delta Theta concerning admission to the party in question was not conceived or devised with the purpose of categorical discrimination attested to by the fact that whites and Negroes were charged to enter the party and that both whites and Negroes entered without charge." However, "several factors convince us that the policy became the vehicle for categorical discrimination." For instance, it was "more difficult for Negroes to enter the party than whites." Black students who presented I.D. cards could not enter even when offering to pay and white Ithaca High School students were able to enter while black students were not. (Apparently the fraternity had decided to prevent black people from Ithaca from getting in, but had not considered such a policy for Cornell blacks. Some overzealous doorkeepers simply extended the policy to exclude all blacks.)

At the meeting of the Afro-American Society that discussed the issue, members of the first generation of black students led by Tundai presented a statement asking freshmen not to rush. The IFC president and several fraternity leaders attended the meeting. They asked black students not to take drastic action and promised to establish an all-black committee to consult black freshmen during rush. Black students voted not to rush, but several of the second generation, led by Arapa, called a meeting of all freshmen to discuss the boycott anyway.

Although black students never took concrete action against the fraternities, their vigorous response to the Phi Delta Theta incident was due to several factors. Occurring at a time when black power made the black community sensitive to all forms of oppression, the incident became symbolic of discrimination within the greater society. Indeed, they interpreted the prejudice at Phi Delta Theta as nothing more than a softer form of the overt Southern variety. Most importantly, as one black student stated, the occurrence infuriated black men because black women had experienced the most blatant cases of abuse. Some brothers felt that one sister had been given an unwarranted caustic interrogation by the counselor for the fraternity during the trials.

After the Phi Delta Theta incident, black students continued to adopt the black power ideology. During the remainder of the academic year, blacks attended all SNCC-sponsored conferences devoted to black power, particularly those concerned with the manifestation and expression of black power at the college level. Through a joint effort of both the IFC and the Afro-American Society, a Soul Week was held during which many national advocates of black power appeared, including Stokely Carmichael. At this time, black men were permitted to establish a separate all-black dorm for themselves. The establishment of Elmwood House, the name of the black males' coop, amounted to an admission by the university that it had not tried to make life on a white campus palatable to blacks. The fraternities, the hub of the university's social life, had not been able to accept or assimilate large numbers of black men. Consequently, Elmwood relieved the tension between blacks and whites. On the other hand, the founding of Wari, the COSEP female coop, in the spring of 1967, was to have a different impact on the university's racial situation. In this instance, the university believed not only that it had made earnest efforts to improve the racial climate but also that significant racial progress had been made. The demand for a COSEP female cooperative shattered the university's sense of gradually improving racial relations. Unlike Elmwood, Wari's establishment exacerbated racial tensions. Indeed, as we shall see later, if Wari had not existed, one of the more important reasons for precipitating the occupation of Willard Straight Hall could not have occurred.

Dai's tenure of office, 1967–68, as president of the Afro-American Society represents the ascendancy of the second-generation blacks and culminates with the division of the Afro-American Society into its three important factions. Although the first two presidents for the Society had been of the Yippie first generation, Dai's rise to power was something less than a coup d'état for his generation. Actually Afro-American Society members had elected a Yippie first-generation member as president and Dai as vice president for the 1967–68 academic year. But when the president-elect decided not to return to Cornell during the fall semester, Dai took over the vacated position.

During his freshman year, 1966–67, Dai held office as chairman of the membership committee. A diligent worker, he had used this position to establish himself as the most militant black on campus. Dai did not hesitate to point out that he had credentials, for he had worked with SNCC in

New York in the campaign against the draft and the war. It did not matter that his role with SNCC had been a minor one, for most black students at Cornell had not done as much. A government major who studied under Professors Berns and Sindler, Dai would get visibly upset if you suggested that perhaps he had been unduly influenced by them. On the other hand, he got some satisfaction from knowing that most members of the Government Department were proud of his academic progress. A successful COSEP student, Dai would often cite his own case as an example of the fact that standardized test scores were poor forecasters of academic success.

At Cornell, Dai increased his knowledge of the Marxist philosophy, which he had acquired in the anti-war campaign. At times he encountered great difficulty trying to unite Marxism with black power. The former transcended race and emphasized the class nature of the struggle against oppression, while the latter subordinated the class conflict to the overwhelming fact of race and the oppression of the third world people, especially Afro-Americans. As one student, a Yippie, stated, "A man less snobbish, less self-assured, less dogmatic, would have given up in depair" when confronted with the challenge inherent in the synthesis of Marxism and black power.

Although the Afro-American Society began to factionalize, it did not disintegrate because Dai held it together by the tight, personal way in which he ran the organization. Yet, although he suppressed the factionalization within the organization, Dai could not provide channels through which the tendency to factionalize could be expressed and resolved. Consequently, instead of engaging in vigorous debates during Society meetings, the various factions convened clandestinely within the homes of their respective leaders. Under such circumstances the splintering of the AAS was accelerated rapidly.

Since he had been the leader of the militant second generation, most of whom later formed the membership of the Radicals, Dai should have allied himself with that faction, but he was prevented by his involvement with Marxism, his maverick-like independence, his attempt to serve as an impartial president, and his attachment to the Government Department. Eventually Dai's own followers went beyond their original leader and developed a militancy of their own.

Ndbizu, a member of the first generation selected to replace Dai in the spring presidential election of 1968, was a relatively uninspiring person. Apparently secure in his moderate political posture, Ndbizu can be described as an independent who lacked the enthusiasm and the desire for leadership. In fact, his election had occurred because of the vigorous efforts of the black women, mainly second generation, who were primarily reacting to Dai's leadership. Dai had accepted unquestioningly the notion implicit in the works of such writers as Elkins, Moynihan, and others that black women were traditionally the dominant figures within the black community. Reacting against this image of male-female relationship in the black community, Dai subconsciously relegated black women to a subordinate role within the Afro-American Society. He did not allow them to hold important positions, nor did he permit them to participate in the formulation of the organization's ideology. For black women similarly influenced by the liberal sociological conception of the black community, Dai's assertion of manhood as expressed in the way he subordinated them was a good and honorable thing. But for women who considered themselves the intellectual equals of men, self-subordination came hard. In effect, Ndbizu's election represented the role-confusion that develops in the upward-mobile black women and men educated by whites who do not understand the distinctive character of the Afro-American experience.

Our society possesses almost unlimited capacity to absorb the rhetoric of new ideas. At one level this involves commercializing the rhetoric and co-opting the rhetoricians; at another it requires declaring the rhetoric off limits and eliminating or destroying the exponents of the new ideologies. As in the larger society, Cornell students and liberal faculty moved at first to co-opt the militants and their cause. That is, they decided to allow them the forms but not the substance of their militancy. The university community rapidly learned the militant new vocabulary and eagerly sought the expertise of the militant on all matters relevant to the black community.

No doubt the act of haranguing whites, which characterized such consultations, had the initial effect of creating a vehicle for the release of the frustrations blacks experienced while living in a university environment that was hostile to their cultural needs. The implicit "children will be children" notion involved in the tolerance of the black students' verbal attack on the system was accepted by all but the most conservative members of the university. They either took blacks more seriously or held onto the old child-rearing idea that children must be disciplined. In fact, the rising level of verbal militancy within the Afro-American Society coincided with the intensification of black frustration. This frustration grew because blacks knew that whites enjoyed the punishment, indeed, they enjoyed it to the point of not actually taking blacks seriously. Blacks began to feel that they were entertaining rather than educating the university community. Black frustration increased because whites, by enjoying the punishment, deprived blacks of the therapeutic value inherent in the act of punishing.

If the higher level of frustration were given political rather than emotional expression, black students would be extremely dangerous. Otherwise, unguided and undirected, the increased frustration increased the likelihood that blacks would be co-opted, since the simple absorption of the new militancy by the whites seemed to instruct blacks in the futility of attempting to change or destroy the system. But two events occurring in the spring of 1968 challenged black students to seek the substance of black power. Both were interrelated;

both were important to the later development of black students. One was the McPhelin incident and the other was a move to establish black studies on the campus.

During the spring semester of 1968 Professor McPhelin taught a basic economics course. The black students who took the course charged that the instructor made prejudicial statements about black people. The Afro-American Society, bringing the issue before the economics faculty, asked that the instructor be fired and insisted on being allowed equal time to rebut some of the allegations made by McPhelin. The Economics Department supported the privilege of the professor to give a course in any manner he desired and refused to comply with the black students' request. Believing that there were limits to professorial prerogative, black students responded by sitting in the Economics Department until their requests were met.

The McPhelin incident demonstrated the racist character of the university and impressed upon them the necessity of establishing courses that would be relevant to their requirements. In another sense, the failure of academia to meet the needs of blacks, as reflected in that incident, and the subsequent demands of black students for black studies programs, illustrate the strategy of adjustment and accommodation inherent in black power. An illustration exists in the nature of the jury system and its effect on black people. In Mississippi, when a white man murders a black man he is not convicted of the crime. There the jury system, through the doctrine of a jury of peers, makes it possible for a Ku Klux Klan defendant to be tried by a Ku Klux Klan jury. Composing the minority of the population, blacks cannot reshape the jury system short of force or intervention by a third party such as the federal government. What they can do is demand that the doctrine of a jury of peers be extended to apply in cases where a black man is a defendant. Thus, when a black man shoots a white man who attempts to burn his home or rape his daughter, he will be tried by a jury of his peers. This tactic constitutes a militant posture of accommodation intended primarily to insure the survival of the black community and secondarily to prepare for the uplifting of that community by allowing time to prepare for an attack on the system.

The demand for black studies was analogous to the situation of black Mississippians demanding a part in the jury system. As a small segment of the university community, blacks could not change the educational process without resorting to force or the help of a third party. The McPhelin incident demonstrated the futility of expecting people with a stake in the system to change that system. Consequently, the black students sought to create a structure within the university community where the notion of professorial privilege would serve the black community. They wanted a program where black professors could teach black ideology, just as, in their view, white professors reflected the dominant ideology of their society. Like the demands of the black Mississippians to have the benefits of the jury system extended to the black community, the demands of black students for black studies programs at Cornell were intended to provide primarily for the psychological survival of black students enrolled in white universities and secondarily to prepare those students to contribute to the uplifting of their community. Later, however, black students learned that, for blacks, survival could not be distinguished from uplifting and furthermore that, for blacks, the act of survival was itself a revolutionary action.

Following the McPhelin incident, the university administration and black students began to investigate the possibility of developing courses on the black experience. From these discussions, the idea emerged that a program of studies eventually offering a major and a minor should be developed to deal specifically with the Afro-American experience. Black students liked the idea because the establishment of a program amounted to an admission by the university that blacks had peculiar sets of problems and experiences that were radically different from those of white society. Furthermore, they felt that such a program emphasized that the United States' relationship to black people was similar to its relationship to other third world peoples. Thus blacks frequently compared their program to those on Latin America, Africa, and Asia. The university administration seemed to like the idea of a program because it constituted an expression of its sensitivity to the problems of black students on the white campus.

During much of the spring semester 1968, black students were influenced by moderate thought and predisposed to work for a program that was not completely separatist or autonomous. They initiated meetings with several professors to discuss courses that might be offered by the various departments. Since most meetings were held on Sunday, most professors invited to the meetings were often too busy to come, did not stay long, or attended the sessions infrequently. In the beginning the most enthusiastic support for the idea of black courses came from the Government and History Departments (whose offices, incidentally, were located in the same building) because militant graduate and undergraduate black students in those departments made a special effort to enlist their support.

Substantive discussions during these meetings moved on two levels of thought. At one level black students displayed an interest in establishing relevant courses and in providing for black student input in the development of those courses, while the professors expressed a concern for establishing legitimate courses and for maintaining academic standards. At another level, blacks wanted the department to hire black professors to teach the courses, while the university professors were immediately concerned with devising ways in which existing faculty could be utilized until blacks could be found. Thus in the initial stages of the program the fundamental issues about black studies were raised. But more importantly, black students in their assessment of which professors might support their ideas soon discovered that they had very few friends on the faculty.

When it was found at the end of the term that no substantial progress had been made in the development of a black studies program, the university administration appointed Chandler Morse, a liberal, middle-aged, respected professor of economics, to head a committee to explore ways in which a program might be established. The Morse appointment represents the administration's first major mistake. In terms of administration and faculty interest, Morse had two faults: he believed in student power, and he was prone to admit his ignorance of what should constitute a program of Afro-American studies. This meant that he tended to approach black students at a level of absolute equality when it came to their input in the development of black studies. Later, when he was very critical of Ndbizu's actions, Dai, who had worked on the original committee and who generally believed confused people should be told what to do, charged that Morse had been too permissive and that such permissiveness showed a lack of interest in black studies. In fact, Morse had been the only professor interested enough to accept the position of chairman of the Committee on Afro-American Studies. In one sense, the Morse appointment was the best thing that could have happened to black students. His behavior forced blacks to develop a program for themselves. In particular, his actions pulled the Radicals, who had given up on black students, back into the Afro-American Society, for now they had the opportunity to use a program to politicize and radicalize black students and to institutionalize their ideological perspective.

The initial contest for control of the Afro-American Society erupted, after a meeting in early October of 1968, into a fight between the major factions. Saddened and shocked by what happened, black students during the week ahead sought an explanation for their behavior. They concluded that the Afro-American studies program was not to blame for what had occurred and consequently should not be abandoned in order to unify the organization. Instead they fixed responsibility for their behavior on the racist nature of the Cornell community, on the actions of Chandler Morse, on the university administration, and on themselves. Believing that the immediate problem of establishing internal unity could best be solved with and after the expulsion of whites from all activities impinging upon black people, the major factions decided to remove all whites from the Afro-American Studies Committee.

The self-criticism generated by the open conflict that had occurred was expressed in the way black students criticized the Society's leadership. Many Afro-American Society members believed that black leadership had to perform two functions: it had to deal with the white society; it had to lead in the improvement of the black community. When black leaders failed to serve either of the two functions, they became illegitimate. In terms of their own experience, black students at Cornell felt that their leadership had not dealt properly with whites in the negotiations over black studies. Furthermore, their leaders had not preserved the essential unity of the Afro-American Society. Both failures had left the organization vulnerable to attack and destruction. Consequently, the question of the old leadership's legitimacy could be raised.

However, illegitimate leadership is not necessarily illegal leadership. The first depends more or less on the power to coerce mentally, while the second relies on accepted procedures for the use of physical coercion. Black students lacked confidence in their old leaders, but there existed no procedure in their constitution for recalling them. Having no legal recourse for removing officers, the only alternative remaining seemed to be an internal coup d'état. But those black students who aspired to control the Society knew that such a drastic step might provoke black students to question the *organization's* legitimacy. Obviously, it was pointless to lead an organization that black students no longer accepted.

The Radical-Convert coalition dealt with the problems posed by illegitimate leadership in the following manner. First, they made careful distinctions between the Afro-American Society and its Negotiating Committee on Afro-American Studies. Secondly, they succeeded in getting Zimbawa elected to spearhead the negotiations with the administration. With these steps, the coalition placed itself in position to seize *effective* control of the Afro-American Society. As the issue of Afro-American studies consumed more and more of the black students' time and interest, the position of chairman of the Negotiating Committee grew in importance. Whereas initially he had made reports at regular Society meetings, by December the chairman of the Negotiating Committee would hold special meetings of his own. As attendance at regular Afro-American Society meetings declined and that at the special meetings increased, Zimbawa moved to the forefront in dealing with the university and establishing unity within the Afro-American Society.

In assessing the events surrounding the coalition's take-over of the Afro-American Society one could speculate that if Dai had been chairman the process might not have occurred so easily. Indeed, Dai himself would assert that he never would have let conditions reach the state they did. In fact, Dai's personality would have caused him to treat the situation differently; but more importantly, Ndbizu lacked the concrete political base necessary to prevent a take-over, even if he had tried. Between his election as compromise candidate and the events of October, he had not had the time or the inclination to build such a base. Lacking supporters, Ndbizu could do nothing but acquiesce in the coalition's ascending influence.

When the Radical-Convert coalition began negotiating with the university administration, most black students tended to approve of the university's efforts to establish a black studies program. In order to bring the black brother to actively criticize the administration, the coalition intensified its criticism of what the Committee on Afro-American Studies had done. Specifically the coalition charged that the old Committee on Afro-American Studies had been deliberately ambiguous in its reporting of the funds allotted to the Afro-American Studies Program. Eventually, after black students had developed a radical view of what constituted a black studies program, the coalition launched a new attack on the administration. After a week of discussion, on Friday, December 6, representatives of the Afro-American Society led by coalition leaders entered a regularly scheduled meeting of the Committee on Afro-American Studies. They stated that the Committee was abolished, that an all-black Afro-American Institute had been formed, and that all Afro-American Studies funds were to be turned over to black students by Monday. On Monday, December 8, black students escalated their demands by including the idea of a college instead of an institute and by listing some of their immediate needs. Unfortunately, black students set a deadline, December 10, for an affirmative response from the university administration.

The President's response on Wednesday, December 10, to the black students' demands represents a classical application of the divide and conquer theory, which almost worked. He accepted most of the immediate demands of the Afro-American Society. He reaffirmed the university's continuing interest in developing an Afro-American Studies Program with and for black students, but he rejected the idea of an autonomous all-black college. In effect then, Perkins substituted for the Afro-American Society's proposal one of his own. It was a substitute that, regardless of its merits, amounted to a rejection of the Afro-American Society's proposal.

As a liberal crisis-manager, Perkins gave his best performance. The Perkins proposal seemed calculated to force a confrontation from black students. "Presumably the next step was theirs," a *Cornell Daily Sun* reporter wrote at the end of one of his commentaries on Perkins' actions. Although growing increasingly more frustrated, the white community still expressed sympathy with Perkins' actions. The Board of Trustees gave him complete support and the faculty reminded him that he had to do something. Furthermore, Perkins knew that most black students were not as radical as the Afro-American Society's leadership, and he responded in such a way as to make that leadership look irresponsible. If blacks had responded, even if they had destroyed university property, Perkins would have emerged victorious out of the conflict.

That Wednesday evening black students met for the fourth consecutive night. The largest number of black students to attend a meeting all year packed a room where candles glowed, incense burned, and brothers beat a warm rhythm on drums that Perkins had purchased for the Society. As the music died, Zimbawa began speaking, retelling the story of how far black students had come in the struggle that year. Just as Zimbawa began to make students say where they had to go from there, Brother Tundai, from within the shadows, leaning up against the wall, said, "Last year on the night Martin Luther King died while lying in a ditch, the pigs' bullets whirling over my head, I decided that Ithaca is too small a town to die in."[2] Zimbawa was astonished that Tundai had no plans to challenge the administration's substitute proposal. Black students were relieved, the tension had been broken.

In his explanation Tundai almost said explicitly that he had deliberately played on their emotions, keying them up to a confrontation he had not planned. All he had wanted to do was prove to the brothers and the sisters that the honkey was no good, and now that this had been proved everyone could go home better prepared to understand the nature of the racists' society. It was a poor excuse which actually made Tundai look worse than he was. Next, the coalition broke down, and the leaders commenced feuding in a way that

[2] Some students reported shootings in skirmishes with whites in the wake of King's murder.—Eds.

made the observers feel as if they really had been guinea pigs. Just as brothers were about to physically confront brothers, Denuru spoke up in an angry commanding voice and told everyone to go home to bed.

Before the meeting broke up, several students announced their intentions to leave Cornell and said that all interested students should meet with them later. About seventy students appeared at the meeting, but most of them did not really intend to leave Cornell, they only wanted someone to offer words of sanity, to pinch them and wake them from a nightmare. Since its take-over the coalition had fed them a steady diet of drums, honkeyisms, and black unity. Now their world had turned down side up as everyone stood isolated and alone. It is impossible to describe what happens when a black dream has been shattered. Only the participant can ever understand the experience, and he should never forget it.

Self-hatred is what most black students felt. Somewhere in the recesses of their minds most of the brothers knew that even if the coalition had held together they probably would not have confronted the honkey. Even worse, they began to feel that failure had been built into their efforts from the very beginning. That night they cursed Tundai for deceiving them, for destroying the unity that had developed over the past month, and for denying them the exercise of their own wills. That night Tundai fell into disfavor until April 21. The next day the black students began to suspect Zimbawa's ideological outlook. If he had been truly revolutionary, they thought, he would have acted without them. Indeed, if he had acted out of convictions, no matter what he thought of black students, he might have politicized them and moved them to act. Zimbawa's influence would not survive this discovery of his Achilles' heel.

In the beginning there was blackness; blackness was Zimbawa, and Zimbawa was radical. A brilliant engineering student and a good chess player, Zimbawa's mind plowed through fertile fields of unconventional thought. Nearly every militant or revolutionary concept known to black Cornellians had issued first from Zimbawa's mouth. To black students, Zimbawa was not super cool, or so super black as to be uncool, rather he was so super cool and super black as to be super serious. The Yippies often said that if Zimbawa slept with only one white woman he would change his ideological perspective. To which the Radicals replied, probably so, but if Zimbawa ever slept with a white woman Zimbawa would not be Zimbawa. In a group of black students where the disease known as blacker-than-thou had not been eradicated completely, Zimbawa was truly black.

A second-generation Radical, Zimbawa had played a major role in the McPhelin incident mentioned earlier. As a student enrolled in the economics courses taught by McPhelin he heard the instructor make such comments as "The Indians were over here for hundreds of years, but nothing worth while was ever done to the land until the white man came," and "The economic condition of black people is generally reflective of their lower life style." Zimbawa told other blacks what McPhelin had said. Some of the first generation who had taken the course the previous term said that the statements had been much worse, and that members of the Economics Department had even found it necessary to caution the professor. Shocked, Zimbawa could not understand how blacks had tolerated such statements. Unlike the first generation, Zimbawa decided that McPhelin's statements called for action, not acquiescence.

After the McPhelin incident Perkins had Zimbawa, along with Arapa and another participant in the Economics Department sit-in, explain to whites the black students' motives for their actions. Although most of the discussion occurred in the Statler Dining Hall, the three black students did not wear jackets and sometimes walked in with sneakers on. Once, after Perkins had commented on their appearance, Zimbawa suggested that he purchase jackets for them. Perkins agreed and bought them blue blazers with Cornell emblems.

The following day the three black students wore the blazers on campus, informing all black students they encountered that they were officially university "niggers" and should be listened to.

One reason why most Afro-American Society members reacted so strongly to the discovery that Zimbawa had a shortcoming lay in the nature of the social relationship that existed between the Radical and most of the Afro-American Society members. At first, Zimbawa's relationship to black women was defined by his youth and by the fact that he did not consider himself handsome. Later the question of the role of black women complicated this primary situation. According to Radical thought, political black women should date only political black men to avoid being corrupted by unpolitical men. Or they should politicize those unpolitical men whom they dated. Unpolitical women should always relate to political men if they wanted to be political. From the Radical viewpoint the other two factions, especially the Yippies, were unpolitical. The Radicals had a small cadre of women, but the other two factions, particularly the Yippies, had the largest number of women. The Radicals believed that the political black woman not only was unable to politicize her lesser political brother, but actually was being corrupted by him. Consequently, while they understood why an unpolitical woman might be attracted to an unpolitical man, they never saw how a political woman could be. When the black coed did not conform to the ideal model of the black woman, the Radicals concluded that she was unpolitical. When the black female made no effort to change, the Radicals grew more disappointed and angry with her. Upon sensing the attitude of the Radicals, the black woman found it even more difficult to communicate with them and turned more and more to the men in the other two factions. To complicate matters further, the Radicals blamed the Yippies and the Converts for exploiting black women sexually and for not trying to politicize them.

As Radicals' estrangement grew, their dislike for Yippie and Convert men also increased. The Radicals had an impenetrable case against the Yippies, the Converts, and most of the black women. So non-Radical black men and women comforted each other by drawing closer together. From this experience, the Radicals decided that all blacks in the organization were not worth fighting for. Thus Radicals exonerated Zimbawa by saying it was useless for him to waste his good life in a futile effort to change a lot of worthless blacks. Ultimately such an attitude tended to give Zimbawa's assessment of Cornell blacks an unrealistic distortion. More importantly, it led to the discovery of the crucial fault that resulted in his loss of legitimacy.

Tundai's statement in the meeting of December 16, and the black students' reluctance to confront the university, reinforced Zimbawa's negative attitude toward black people. He felt that black students had committed themselves to support their demand. When they did not, he grew more angry with them. Nevertheless, as the organization's leader, he had to unify the badly splintered Society and preserve its image. He found the solution to both problems in a statement prepared by Warema and presented it to the Afro-American Society at their Thursday night meeting.

The statement, which appeared as a letter to James Perkins in the editorial column of the *Cornell Daily Sun,* was, with the exception of the demands, the first official document of the Afro-American Society directed at the Cornell white community. It explained why blacks had come to Cornell, why they wanted a black studies program, and why they had rejected white participation. Furthermore, it dispelled notions that such a program was impossible, reaffirmed the blacks' intentions to persist in their demands, and opened the door for negotiations with the university. For black students the statement, which was read three times at the Thursday meeting, dissolved the confusion of the past few days and inspired them to continue to struggle.

Coming after a long period of almost total silence, the Afro-American Society's statement was eagerly read and analyzed by both the Cornell and Ithaca white community. For whites the statement indicated that the black demands were not designed to destroy the university but were "based on both sincerity and strong emotional involvement." By rejection of violent confrontation when they had the opportunity and "tacit obligation" to use it, black students effectively regained the ears of the white community. The white community congratulated them, not Perkins, for avoiding a crisis.

If blacks had behaved violently in December, Perkins would have won. He could have disciplined them as he wished without tarnishing his liberal image, for the times favored him. If blacks had occupied a building then, their past behavior would have precluded the support of SDS and six thousand white students. By April, both SDS and white students begged blacks to let them participate in the revolutionary structuring of the university. If blacks had confronted Perkins in December, liberalism would have prevailed. By April, liberals would serve as liberalism's pallbearers. If blacks had carried guns in December, we would not be writing about it now. Instead, black students contented themselves with issuing a warning, with toppling over a candy machine, and with brandishing a few toy guns. Unfortunately, blacks could get little satisfaction from what had happened, for they had not planned things that way.

The New Year began with belated efforts by James Perkins to correct his biggest mistake. Throughout the struggle between black students and the university administration in the fall of 1968, the administration had never succeeded in asserting control over the direction of the Afro-American Studies Program. To do this, the administration appointed W. Keith Kennedy as Chandler Morse's replacement on the old fifteen-man Committee on Afro-American Studies. In terms of administration interests, the Kennedy appointment was a wise move made too late. Whereas Chandler Morse had been either too sympathetic to black students or singularly inept at protecting university interests, Kennedy, a university administrator, understood the need to maintain administration and faculty control over black studies. Furthermore, Kennedy's appointment indirectly challenged the power of black students to control the program by implying that the old fifteen-man Committee on Afro-American Studies, which black students had declared defunct, would continue to serve as the main policy-making body for black studies. This became explicit on January 7, 1969, when the Afro-American Society received a letter from the university inviting it to select eight students to serve on the reconstituted Committee on Afro-American Studies.

Perkins' decision to take immediate steps to establish university control over black studies was based on a report made by Professor David Brion Davis, who had attended a fall conference on black studies at Yale University. Davis observed that the Yale administration had played the major role in defining the objectives and setting the limits of its Afro-American Program. Consequently, Yale had already decided that its program would be interdepartmental, with an integrated faculty and offering minors in Afro-American Studies to both black and white students. Such rapid and direct action by the Yale administration had the effect of precluding an opportunity for black students to raise fundamental questions concerning the aim and direction of black studies on the white campus.

Davis' analysis of the reasons why Yale established the kind of program it did is not the only one. One must assume that, whether moderate or radical, whether fully cognizant of what had happened, or deceived by the Yale administration, the blacks there perceived that their program was relevant to them. As long as blacks are not content with a program, no amount of administration strength will make them like it. As long as they do not like it, that program has an uncertain future. In terms of black studies, black students possess the power not only to disrupt but to boycott. But, above all, one should remember that Yale had no black women.

Perkins' move to re-establish the old Committee on Afro-American Studies and his appointment of Kennedy to chair the committee provided another opportunity for black students to confront the university. But with the memory of the December fiasco vivid in their minds, black students were hesitant about engaging the administration in another immediate confrontation. Rather, they chose to withdraw, even at the risk of allowing the administration to gain the initiative, for a period of self-criticism and introspection. But before they did, blacks decided to grant informal recognition to Kennedy as the liaison between the university administration and themselves, for someone had to sign the vouchers paying the blacks who came as consultants on black studies. Second, black students refused to appoint eight members to the old committee.

The move to accept Kennedy as the liaison between the administration and black students was part of an over-all strategy, based upon research that had been done on the operation of the university. This research revealed that although Cornell consisted of a complex of various colleges, some private and some public, most of the opposition to the establishment of the program desired by blacks would come from the College of Arts and Sciences. For one thing, the College of Arts and Sciences regarded itself as guardian of the university tradition; for another, black studies threatened its disciplines more than those of any other college. The research also showed that, while students possessed residual power over the university, the faculty held effective power and the Board of Trustees wielded veto power. To attain effective authority over black studies, black students had to fight the faculty. But the size and diversity of the faculty made it difficult to fix responsibility on any particular group and hence to plan any viable strategy of attack. On the other hand, black students expected opposition from the two major reservoirs of effective faculty power, the prestigious departments and the prestigious faculty members. These two groups would lead the attack on an autonomous black studies program.

Black students tried to avoid a direct challenge to the faculty by resorting to the use of the Board of Trustees' veto power. Perkins had used the tactic to innovate the controversial COSEP program. Black students wanted the Board of Trustees to serve as final arbiters in the disputes between the faculty and themselves. They assumed that Perkins would support their demands either out of sympathy to their cause or under the threatened disruption of the university. Blacks sought to place Perkins in such a position that his career at Cornell depended upon the successful establishment of a black studies program that was acceptable to them. At the same time, blacks desired to make the program independent of Perkins so that its fate did not depend entirely upon him. Their acceptance of Kennedy thus represented an initial step in a plan to focus attention on Perkins.

Black students knew that Perkins held a powerless position and that any apparent power he possessed rested upon his ability to manipulate or manage the various contending groups within the university. To prevent him from managing the Afro-American Society, blacks decided not to let any one individual serve as the organization's spokesman. They set up a Negotiating Committee, with rotating membership, to deal with the administration. They did this to prevent Perkins from isolating individual members for reward or punishment.

Because blacks restricted its members' freedom of action the Negotiating Committee was in fact a negotiating committee. Each of its members had to assume the risk of censure and loss of prestige for any initiative he took. The Negotiating Committee could never discuss issues that had not been thoroughly considered in Society meetings. If a committee member made a wrong decision, the Society repudiated his actions and absolved itself of any obligation to abide by the decision. As expected, the plan confused Perkins.

But the strategy employed to frustrate Perkins reflected the frustration, confusion, and general atmosphere of impotence and distrust that existed within the Afro-American Society. Black students created the rotating Negotiating Committee because of a distrust of their leadership, particularly Zimbawa. Believing that white society would never permit the autonomous revolutionary institution black students wanted, Zimbawa saw all negotiations as preliminary skirmishes before confrontation. Like the long prelude of African music and revolutionary readings which preceded each meeting he led, the negotiations were designed to get uncommitted blacks in the mood for struggle. But most blacks could not believe with such certainty that the university would not grant them what they desired. Consequently, they began to perceive in Zimbawa's behavior a deliberate attempt to insure that his prediction regarding the university's attitude would come true. Zimbawa rather than the university was acting in bad faith. The course Zimbawa offered would lead to a recurrence of the December fiasco, or worse still to the destruction of the Society.

Yet black students could not reject Zimbawa's leadership, for he was a good leader, they felt, and above all he established himself as the epitome of Blackness. A repudiation of Zimbawa, furthermore, would constitute a rejection of one's own self-image and one's aspirations, no matter how ill defined they might be. Instead black students allowed Zimbawa to remain as their leader, but indirectly restricted his area of discretionary power. Thus, they used the Negotiating Committee to negotiate, prohibited members from talking to the press and discussing issues with whites, and held each student responsible for any mistake he made.

While Perkins tried to establish administration control over black studies, black students paused for a moment of self-criticism. However, this criticism did not occur as a group effort, for most individuals tended to identify more readily with a faction. Taking place within the various factions, it reinforced and intensified intragroup hostilities. Under such circumstances, the Afro-American Society seemed doomed to repeat the old pattern for dealing with the university. But two factors prevented a repetition of old patterns: one was the supervision of black students by revolutionaries with credible credentials; the other was the disintegration of the Radical faction.

The black men, not undergraduates, who took over supervision of the Afro-American Society were Harry Edwards, Don Lee, Michael Thelwell, and Cleveland Sellers. Although Harry and Don had arrived on the campus in early September 1968, they had avoided involvement in the Afro-American Society. This non-involvement was a judicious decision since black students had not yet reached the level of frustration that would force them to recognize their own impotence and to seek the advice of others. Rather than using his class as a forum on tactics for confronting the university, Don chose to employ poetry and creative writing to speak to the black students' aspirations. Don reminded blacks of the necessity of redefining the role of black women in the building of the black nation and of making radical changes in American society. By January, Don, through the vehicle of the classroom, and Harry, through informal discussions with black students, had succeeded in communicating to blacks a clearer image of their role.

The approach used by Cleve and Mike represents a classical example of the proper way to move black students. Both had worked with SNCC in the South. Having known each other previously, and using the techniques they had learned while field workers for SNCC, the two men began their politicization of blacks at the first Society meeting they attended. Taking the more militant position of the Radicals, but expressing it with more finesse, Cleve spoke of the irrelevance of black students on white campuses; he argued that working within the Establishment, which the blacks' presence at Cornell symbolized, while claiming to be revolutionaries was not only a contradiction but an absurdity; he suggested that they were searching for a militant method to escape the black community and to integrate into white society. When blacks sought to challenge his ability to expound black ideology, Cleve asked for their credentials. Cleve knew blacks had no choice but to agree with him, for they had used the argument that none of their experiences on the white campus were valid in demanding a black studies program. Blacks began to realize that to talk to Cleve they had to acquire credentials, and this meant that they had to do something.

While Cleve attacked blacks at that Society meeting, Mike sympathized with their plight. He informed them that they could be relevant without leaving the white university. Furthermore, he offered to assist them wherever he could. Initially, moderate blacks turned to Mike, but as they grew more militant they sought Cleve's advice. The barometer of a student's militancy became his position between the two poles represented by Mike and Cleve. Symbolically, one could determine a black brother's militancy by comparing the amount of time he spent shooting Mike's bow and arrow with that he spent riding in Cleve's yellow convertible sports car.

The first step in the disintegration of the Radical faction came when, in late January, Zimbawa announced his intention to resign as leader of the Afro-American Society at its next meeting. But because Zimbawa had a history of threatened resignations behind him, most blacks did not take him seriously. In fact, while growing increasingly frustrated and disappointed with black students, Zimbawa did not want to resign, for fighters never quit or expect to be rejected. However, blacks did not realize the extent to which they had changed their attitude toward Zimbawa. In the past, feeling that no one else in the organization was capable of replacing Zimbawa, black students always gave him a vote of confidence and a mandate to remain as their leader. Thus, the

January resignation, like those before, was designed primarily to restore confidence in Radical leadership. But by January 1969 the December fiasco had done irreparable damage to Zimbawa's image.

The meeting in which Zimbawa had planned to resign opened with the sound of African drums and Zimbawa presiding. Upon seeing Zimbawa in the chair, many blacks felt disappointed. It seemed that Zimbawa would continue to serve as chairman. Then, after all other business had been discussed, Zimbawa reiterated his plans to resign; blacks became deadly serious, as if an impending confrontation was about to take place. After a few moments of silence, followed by a few terse comments between some Converts and Radicals, Arapa spoke and calmly accepted Zimbawa's resignation. He opened the house for the election (all knew that with this election Ndbizu would be officially removed) of chairman of the Afro-American Society. A few minutes later, after Zimbawa had nominated him, Bali became the new chairman of the Afro-American Society. (A week before the meeting, Converts and other moderates had met at Tundai's home to plan a strategy for the removal of Zimbawa. Unfortunately, space does not allow a discussion of that meeting.)

Bali, the new leader of the Afro-American Society, had virtually crawled or leaped out of the woodwork. A six-year Ph.D. student in mathematics, Bali, having studied under Berns, had dreamed of becoming the first black philosopher-mathematician. Long after he had read some revolutionary literature, and indeed, even at the time he led blacks into the Straight, Bali believed that *The Republic,* as taught by Berns, was the world's greatest book. Before his election to the chairmanship of the Afro-American Society, he often remarked, with a good deal of satisfaction, that Berns had taken great pains to co-opt him and to make him aim to become the black Plato. After the Straight, Bali would argue, again with satisfaction, that Berns was one of the few professors on campus who understood the revolutionary implication of the Society's actions and, more importantly, who believed that the black leaders were revolutionaries. He attributed Berns's insight to the fact that Dai, Tundai, and he had studied under Berns.

Bali desired the chairmanship of the Afro-American Society because he believed that there was nothing he could not do. Zimbawa had maintained, for tactical reasons, that black students could not have dialogue with the administration without corrupting their revolutionary position. Bali, like many other blacks, felt that they could and blamed Zimbawa for the organization's difficulties. A third-generation COSEP student, Bali allied with the Converts and other moderates. (The Radicals maintained that he had no choice, for they had given him an undesirable rating and rejected him.)

Although initially uncomfortable around black women, Bali set out in late December to cultivate their friendship. He knew that to gain respect among non-Radical men he had to influence black women. He spent several hours at Wari, where, because of his size and enormous appetite, he earned the title "Baby Huey." There was one politically active black woman in Wari who believed that, except for Zimbawa, no man on campus was intelligent enough to claim superiority over her in any relationship which might develop between them. In Bali she found another black man who was; she fell in love with him, and she became one of the most important reasons for his election.

Although elected Chairman of the Afro-American Society's Philosophy Committee in the spring of 1968, Bali had no developed ideological outlook, except for a Bernsian interpretation of Plato. Indeed he attained the chairmanship of the Afro-American Society by default. The old traditional leadership had too many marks against it. Zimbawa had nominated Bali in jest, for his group secretly thought that Bali would make the new non-Radical coalition look foolish.

There was only one person capable of posing a serious threat to Bali's quest for leadership of the Afro-American

Society. That person, Arapa, was a second-generation COSEP student and had allied originally with that generation in the initial challenge to the first generation's influence on campus. In his freshman year, the fall of 1966, he had attempted to lead the freshmen in a boycott of fraternities, even though the second generation had changed its mind; but he was betrayed by most of the freshmen, Zimbawa included, who decided to support the second generation's decision. Because of this, Arapa left school at the end of the semester. When he returned in the fall of 1967, Arapa joined the second-generation Radicals, even though Dai, his best friend, had begun to pursue an independent course. But, although allied with them, Arapa did not develop the hostilities that characterized the Radicals; while away he had reached the emotional maturity that allowed him to retain his friendship with Dai, black women, and Converts. Respected by all groups, his support made possible the peaceful transfer of power. Later it would play a major role in the decision to occupy the Straight. But Arapa's failure in the fall of 1966 made him fearful of assuming subsequent leadership roles in the organization. Because black students sensed his fears, they too were reluctant to thrust positions upon him.

When Bali took office, his position forced him to develop a militant political ideology. His chief asset in helping him to adjust to the demands of the position was his willingness to listen and to take advice. By doing this, he won the aid of the non-Radicals. He permitted those who felt that he was not as "political" as they to believe that they exercised, by giving him advice, de facto control of the Society. Yet he avoided giving Society members the impression that he functioned as a pawn of others by interpreting his advisers in a style distinctly his own and expanding on their ideas wherever he could.

An illustration of Bali's ability to adjust was the way he won the allegiance of Denuru. One evening Bali, Denuru, and Warema met for a beer party. During the evening Denuru, who had spent some time at West Point Military Academy before enrolling in Cornell, began displaying his expertise on the use of guns. Bali proved his equal, so much so that thereafter Denuru and Bali spent the entire evening challenging each other. Later Warema informed Bali that he ought not to have equaled Denuru at every challenge. Such an action, Warema said, made Denuru, who was a Radical, impossible to convert to the non-Radical cause. Bali replied that to earn Denuru's respect and support he had to beat him. Warema responded that the encounter that evening had reduced the significance of the role that only Denuru could play. Furthermore, Warema pointed out that now was the appropriate time to win Denuru's support because he had begun to spend most of his time with one of the black women on campus, rather than with the Radicals. Bali accepted the advice and appointed Denuru to plan the strategy for the occupation of the Straight. (Once inside the Straight, Bali told Warema, "You see, I let Denuru do his thing, and it hasn't made me look bad. In fact, it makes me look good.")

Actually the fact that Denuru dated a black Cornellian was not so much a cause as a result of his rejection of the Radicals. Like other students, he had grown disappointed with Zimbawa's leadership. A brilliant tactician whose first loyalty was to the best interests of the Cornell black community, he had allied first with the Yippies and then with the Converts before joining the Radicals. But he began to feel that Zimbawa had underrated and condescended to black students when it came to their ideological development. Acknowledging the sincerity and consistency of Zimbawa's actions, Denuru nevertheless perceived that they alienated blacks more than they united them. Like Cleve, with whom he had spent a lot of time and who had considerable influence on his ideological development, he saw that no matter how "together" Zimbawa was, he had to be replaced or he might destroy the organization. Deciding that the non-Radical coalition offered a more creative alternative for the solution of the Society's problems, he gave his support to them. His support significantly aided the non-Radical cause, for Denuru, who in contrast to Arapa commanded rather than persuaded, proved a major factor in the successful seizure of Willard Straight Hall.

Following Bali's election, the disintegration of the Radicals came with increasing rapidity. On one occasion, a Radical collared President Perkins. Although his act discredited them, the Radicals' response deserves noting. At the Society meeting at which the issue was discussed, blacks claimed the exclusive right to determine the brother's fate while condemning the act. But they decided to postpone the question of punishment until the administration stated its position. Just before the meeting ended, the errant Radical said that he expected the organization's support because "I did a revolutionary thing." The Radicals, led by Zimbawa, were incredulous. After the meeting the Radicals took the brother into the hallway and read him out of the group.

A few weeks later, Zimbawa left school. The only person capable of replacing him was a freshman who lacked the needed experience. When Zimbawa departed, the non-Radical coalition assumed uncontested control. The non-Radicals, composed of the Converts, Dai, Arapa, Bali, and other moderates, enjoyed the faith of Society members. Everything that the Radicals had been prohibited from doing, the non-Radical coalition was permitted to do. But in terms of the waste of black talent the Afro-American Society had paid a tremendous price. Furthermore, to prove that unity did exist, blacks had to do what disunity had prevented them from doing in December 1968.

The most remarkable fact about the occupation of Willard Straight Hall was James Perkins' surprise at its occurrence. According to the Associated Press releases a few hours after the take-over, Perkins expressed disbelief at what had happened, particularly in the light of the fact that blacks and the university had recently worked out a mutually satisfactory agreement concerning the establishment of an Afro-Ameri-

can Studies Program. Yet Perkins' shock becomes under-
standable when one considers the frame of mind in which
he had approached the subject of black students on campus.
Perkins recognized that blacks represented a new constituency
on a predominantly white campus, but he apparently believed
that their presence did not pose a threat to the basic structure
of the university community. He expected blacks to make
some adjustments to their new environment, and that the
community would adapt itself to the blacks. As chief steward
of the university, Perkins exhibited a readiness to make the
concessions that would aid blacks in acclimating themselves
to their new environment. Blacks, behaving in good faith,
were expected to accept these concessions and take a flexible
attitude toward the university community.

Perkins held the idea that the granting of concessions would
come after open frank discussion growing out of specific
issues. In resolving the conflict between the demands of blacks
for immediate change in the environment and the university
community's opposition to drastic change, discussion would
serve as the major method. During the first and part of the
second semester of the academic year, the specific issue
around which this discussion took place had been black
studies. Extensive negotiations had occurred. They had the
overtones of a game in which the contending teams played
with different rule books. If at times black students had not
followed the rules of proper debate and inquiry, if at times
they had used toy guns and insulted a president, it was because, in his view, they were children, not black men interested in producing revolutionary change.

The notion that blacks played the game badly because they
were children, who had not matured in the art of gamesman-
ship, explains the administration's constant obsession with
the selection of the new director. Whereas the Afro-American Society officially maintained that the studies program had
to be developed before a director could be hired, the administration consistently argued that the director had to be se-

lected first and the program organized around him. The AAS wanted to develop their program. It would define all the program's internal and external relationships, including the role of the director. The administration said that it would be unfair to design a program, when its success would depend to a great degree upon the director, without his participation. Moreover, the administration argued that the faculty would not allow it.

An explanation of why the Afro-American Society wanted to develop a program before the selection of a director and why the administration opposed the idea is found in the AAS's backstage activities surrounding the constitution that it presented to the administration in December 1968. After his appointment to draw up a constitution for a College of Afro-American Studies, Warema wrote the working model of a constitution that attempted to camouflage the organization's radical concepts behind the foliage of traditional academic rhetoric. He presented the model to his committee which, Radical-dominated, rewrote it almost entirely. The model, which would have passed a sympathetic OEO anti-discrimination inspection, assumed that, given the presence of revolutionary leadership, all the AAS's revolutionary ideas, such as the exclusion of whites, would be maintained. As articulated by the Radicals on the committee, however, the model was not enough for the AAS. The constitution had to *guarantee* that a revolutionary leadership would always exist—not simply make it environmentally *possible* for the revolutionary to act.

The motives explaining why Warema wrote the model constitution the way he did, and why the Radicals rejected it, deserve further observation. Warema, who did not identify with any particular faction in this Society, believed that all the blacks in the organization were basically revolutionary. He wrote the constitution so that, once revolutionaries gained control, they could perpetuate themselves in power. His committee, because it was controlled by Radicals who were then antagonistic to the other factions, refused to believe that AAS members were basically revolutionary. In fact, believing that very few blacks were revolutionary, they were uncertain as to whether the revolutionary position would even gain the *initial* control.

In the constitution, furthermore, black students possessed some actual and all the residual control over the college. Warema had provided for student control because he felt that the contemporary blacks would socialize all future blacks in the revolutionary ideology. The Radicals on the committee saw only that the few revolutionaries on the campus would be inundated by a growing number of unpoliticized blacks. Moreover, since the college's faculty would be selected by members of the AAS who he thought were revolutionary enough to select good men, Warema gave faculty members complete control over their curricula in the model constitution. The Radicals on the committee disagreed.

Warema wrote the elaborate document for several reasons, all of which were unacceptable to the Radicals on the committee. Assuming that a revolutionary outlook existed among blacks on campus, Warema was prepared to play the game of designing a detailed document without fear of weakening the revolutionary position. On the other hand, the Radicals on the committee admitted the weakness of the revolutionary viewpoint. They claimed that the organization would lose because it was the white man's game and he had devised an unbeatable system for winning. The Radicals said that blacks could not beat the white man at his own game unless they were prepared to break the rules whenever necessary. Again Warema argued that, since the constitution was an excellent document for revolutionaries to manipulate, its rejection by them was, in fact, an admission that Cornell blacks were not revolutionary. The Radicals on the committee astutely rebutted this by saying that their refusal to abide by the white man's rules, as was the case in not giving the university an elaborate constitution, represented the finest example of a revolutionary act.

Ultimately the Radicals scrapped Warema's model and drew up a constitution that said nothing except that blacks and the director of the college would define all relationships. They included the director because they felt that they had to meet the minimum request of the administration in order to get the black college. They hoped, however, to have most important relationships defined before the selection of the director. His selection, in fact, would be an indication of the college's ideological posture. Warema's constitution defined relationships on the assumption that the blacks knew what they wanted, and he could express those desires. The Radicals assumed nothing and did not define. Perhaps they knew that they could not institute their position, nor could they select a director of their choice, and believed that the Converts might. Within the context of the factionalism existing in the AAS in December, Warema's document would have been counterrevolutionary.

As reflected in the actions of the Radicals on the constitution committee, the AAS's leadership, composed primarily of Radicals, would have wanted a director before the establishment of the college if they could have been sure of his ideological position. But they could not be certain that the AAS, whose ideological commitment to radical change they did not trust, would select the right individual. Their repeated failures had demonstrated that they themselves could not trick, cajole, or force blacks to make the appropriate choice. At the same time, they did not trust the university's intentions in desiring a director right away. The university, the Radicals felt, desired a director in order to exert indirect control over the black students. Theoretically, as the greater society would not allow Cornell University to exist as a revolutionary institution, so Cornell, as an Establishment institution, would not permit a truly revolutionary college or program to exist within its framework. Logically, they maintained, if the university could not have a revolutionary program, they could not be expected to hire a revolutionary director.

With hindsight it is possible to understand the thrust of

the Radical argument. Blacks were concerned about relevant education. In the integrationist period, blacks on a white campus constituted the highest act of commitment to the black community. Those integrationists became the vanguard, whether at the University of Alabama or at the Woolworth lunch counter, of the black struggle for survival and uplift. The black community bestowed upon these students the badge of courage because they bore the scars of police clubs and the stench of rotten eggs on their bodies. On the Northern white campus these integrationists, the "firsters" as the barrier-breakers were labeled, engaged themselves in the battle to destroy the stereotypes that whites used to justify oppression of the black community. Following the development of black separatism, this old vanguard was declared irrelevant, and in one brief moment the revolutionaries of the old era became the counterrevolutionaries of the new.

Given the existence of the new order, black students on white campuses sought ways to make themselves relevant to their community. The Radicals argued that they ought to leave the university as the SNCC members had left the Negro institutions in the days of integration. If they remained, they should constantly *heighten the contradictions,* that is, they ought to raise and prove, through word and deed, that integration had not worked for the black community and could only result in the alienation of a Negro elite from their black brothers. To avoid this, blacks had constantly to make the integrationists' life unpleasant for themselves and the white community. Tactically this could be done through the process known as *confrontation.*

Implicit in the way they used the technique was the assumption that an individual, particularly one who is not highly politicized, rarely consciously acts contrary to his own self-interest. Consequently, the radicals desired to *raise the level of awareness* by heightening the contradiction through the process of confrontation. That is, they wanted blacks to redefine self-interest so that it would become indistinguish-

able from identification with the black community, and so
that it would lead blacks to reject Cornell. Simultaneously,
Radical ideology combined the objective of raising the level
of awareness among blacks with another objective, the destruction of the university—if not its complete destruction, at
least its disruption. Once a black student had become aware
of the contradictions inherent in his presence on the white
campus, reflected on the contradictions inherent in the presence of black people within the racist American society, he
was expected to continue participating in the process of confrontation in order to raise the level of awareness of his less
politicized brother, and to disrupt and destroy the society.
It could even be said that Radical ideology made the process
of disruption and destruction indistinguishable from the process of raising the level of awareness.

The Radicals at Cornell believed that the heightening of
the contradiction through the process of confrontation would
result in the ejection of blacks from the white campus. Un-
consciously, they created situations in which their predictions
seemed to come true. That is, most black students reacted
in this manner to everything they did. On the other hand,
although the Converts used the same rhetoric as the Radicals,
they did not mean the same thing. They advocated heightening the contradiction, the process of confrontation, raising
the level of awareness, and disrupting and destroying the
university; but they could not bring themselves to accept the
consequence of the argument that all these would ultimately
result in their expulsion from the campus. The Converts
were careful never to state the probability of expulsion in
their action. Because the larger society outside the university
was just as oppressive as the Cornell environment, they saw
no point in leaving the latter for the former. Where, they
asked, was the revolutionary structure that would receive
them? Everywhere one lived, they argued, one had to attempt
to work for the survival and uplifting of blacks. Conceding
that they lacked the skill that was needed in the black

community, the Converts asked how they could be relevant by returning to the black community in the same condition as when they left. Furthermore, students who left would only be replaced by others—less politicized or uncommitted blacks. Within the racist establishment they could serve as conduits through which knowledge and information about the enemy could be channeled to the black community. They could send money and material to less advantaged blacks elsewhere.

The Converts differed with the Radicals over the question of whether a director should be chosen before the establishment of the structure. A director with proven credentials could be extremely helpful to the establishment of a revolutionary structure and in aiding students in their ideological development. In many instances, the Converts used the same argument as the university to explain their desire for selecting a director right away. Probably more than anything else, the Converts saw in the selection of a director a chance to wrest control from the Radicals. If their opinion was given a chance for expression, they felt certain of its triumph. A fair and impartial director would at least allow this. Ultimately, as we shall see, the selection of the director would coincide with the ascendancy of the Convert-dominated, non-Radical coalition.

Whatever the administration's reasons for desiring a director, James Turner's selection did improve the dialogue between the blacks and the administration. Until he arrived, the administration never seemed quite to understand what blacks wanted. To faculty, students, and alumni, the university had constantly described a program very similar to the Yale model. The administration never seemed to accept the notion that blacks really wanted a completely autonomous program, open only to black students and staffed only by black professors. While black students made these ideas explicit, the blandness with which they expounded them made the ideas seem childish. But Turner could talk the administration's language without compromising the blacks' position, a fact that, incidentally, the Radicals believed impossible.

A beautiful illustration of Turner's impact on negotiations between black students and the administration over the Afro-American Studies Program was his first official meeting with university officials. During this session, members of the Radical faction demanded to know from the university, in simple yes or no terms, whether their demands for a black college would be met. When the university did not respond immediately, some Radicals issued several threats and walked out of the room. Turner, however, remained with a few other black students to explain the black students' position. After Turner finished, one administration official exclaimed, "But they never told us this!" From that point on, Turner became a necessity, for he could talk the administration's language. A few weeks later, the Black Studies Program was finalized.

When black students seized the student union, the issue of black studies was practically dead. Indeed, an article had appeared earlier in the Sunday supplement of the New York *Times* that described the Cornell situation to everyone's satisfaction. In it, blacks looked militant, Perkins looked liberal, and Cornell looked good. The alumni responded so favorably to the article that Perkins privately informed Turner that the original budget for the program might be revised to include all the items desired by the black students.

The occupation of Willard Straight Hall was another violation of the rules of the game, but Perkins did not panic; realizing that the crisis ought not to have occurred, he set out to manage it. The new crisis was simply another inning of the same game. This time, however, Perkins made two errors: he did not surround Willard Straight and he permitted blacks to leave the Straight with arms (which, some charged, he should never have allowed within the building). Both mistakes made him play the game badly; both, I suggest, grew from his particular perception of the minds of black students.

Perkins consistently maintained that the AAS represented

one segment of the black population. Eventually, some hundred students were in the union building; they represented the known quantity; he could isolate them, but he could never be sure of the hundred and fifty or more black students who had not entered the building. In order to avoid having black students who were not in the Straight unite in support of those within, Perkins had to act swiftly without antagonizing those inside or outside. In fact, Perkins had to consider the two thousand black citizens of Ithaca. To determine their attitude, he contacted Mayor Kieley, who took him to the home of one prominent Ithacan. When asked by Perkins what he felt about the situation on the hill, the black man stated that if forced to make a decision he would support the black brothers in the building. Perkins decided that surrounding the Straight with police officers might antagonize the black community as much as it would protect or isolate the blacks who were occupying the building. Indeed, perhaps overly cautious, Perkins went so far as to allow any black person free access in entering or leaving the student union.

Second, Perkins knew that there were at least two factions within the AAS. Although the moderate faction led by Bali had organized the take-over, members of the more militant faction had also participated. If Perkins acted too slowly or surrounded the building with police officers, the militants would gain control, with disastrous results for the university. When black students brought guns into the Straight, the situation became more dangerous. Furthermore, whereas he might safely assume that Bali's group would respect the use of guns, he could not be as certain about the militant faction. In telephone conversations with Bali he learned that, while moderates still led the organization, the growing restlessness of the students might change that situation at any moment. On the basis of limited knowledge, he decided to get black students out as quickly as possible *without bloodshed*.

The fact that Perkins was aware that the AAS had a moderate group and a militant group becomes extremely im-

portant in explaining why he allowed blacks to leave Willard
Straight Hall with guns. The statements the moderates issued
to explain why and how they had brought guns to Willard
Straight were revealing. Those statements, released shortly
after the occupation, said: "It was this frustration on our
part and racism on the university's part that forced us to
constantly move forward in this direction." Speaking of the
activities of December 1968, the Society reported, "It was
the consensus at that time that our action would be non-
violent." "We were not armed when we entered the building,
we did not expect to be attacked since we were so meticulous
about being non-violent ourselves." Their "initial manner was
one of urgency but also one of non-violence." And they
"began to improvise weapons for [our] defense." "Historically
the white boy has made the black woman a target of racism
and inhumanity. No longer will we allow our women to be
harmed in any fashion by this white boy." "The real issues
here are of social justice for black people."

Frustration, non-violence, women, social justice, and self-
defense are explanations that white men, not African savages,
are reputed to give to justify the use of weapons. Indeed, the
gun itself is construed to be a white weapon, and the fact
that black students used it, not knives, to defend noble ideas
was a persuasive argument to Perkins that they were civilized.
Perkins did not fear moderate black students with guns because, like Kenneth M. Stampp before him, he saw them as
little more than white men or children in black skins.[3] The
major assumption behind Perkins' organization of the COSEP
program and behind his concession to help blacks adjust to
their environment was that ultimately their needs and aspirations were not unlike those of white students. He probably
found the scene of black students with guns no more disturbing than a similar scene of white young Democrats. His

[3] In his study of American slavery, *The Peculiar Institution* (1956),
Stampp says: "I have assumed that the slaves were merely ordinary
human beings, that innately Negroes are, after all, only white men
with black skins, nothing more, nothing less" (viii).—Eds.

readiness to play games and his failure to provide an atmosphere conducive to black people were consequences of his belief that blacks were not uniquely different from whites.

This does not mean that Perkins believed that all Africans were civilized. He did believe in the possibility, indeed the necessity, of their conversion, and above all he could *distinguish* between Africans. I suggest that if Zimbawa had led the occupation of Willard Straight Hall, Perkins would have behaved differently. Perkins saw Zimbawa as intelligent but irrational, hostile and uncompromising. Bali was intelligent and understanding; moreover he lived in Telluride (honors society house). With Zimbawa or his faction in control Perkins would have surrounded the Straight with officers and probably would have opened fire on black students with the least provocation.

In the four weeks following the events of April 21, Perkins spent most of his time trying to convince others that the natives had not been rebellious, but that frustrated white youths in black skins had acted non-violently in the name of womanhood, social justice, and self-defense. The typical response is illustrated in a cartoon sent Dean Gloria Joseph, Assistant Dean for Student Affairs in charge of COSEP. The cartoon is a hand-drawn sketch of a big-lipped, kinky-haired, bone-jowled, potbellied black man who, dressed in a grass skirt and holding a spear, stirs a black pot with James Perkins and Cornell University boiling inside. President Perkins failed to persuade most Americans, like the sender of the cartoon, because most Americans saw nothing more dangerous than restless natives who had guns in their hands. Above all, within this society guns are symbols of manhood. If whites had accepted Perkins' perceptions, it would have meant that they recognized the manhood of blacks. Consequently, they would have been obligated to alter drastically their treatment of the black students. Perkins' failure was the failure of liberalism in a community and society where liberalism can only play the role of prostitute.